Well Isle Beef Hooked, I Own A Racehorse!

By

Ivan R Don

&

Fannif Art

Copyright © Owen Publishing

All rights reserved

The moral right of Owen Publishing to be identified as the author of this book has been asserted by them in accordance with the Copyright, Designs and Patents Act 1988

First published in 2024

No parts of this book may be reproduced or transmitted in any form or by any means without permission from the publisher.

On behalf of and in memory of

Graham Patterson

1967 – 2023

Special thanks to Billy for his input and for his help in putting this book together. Thanks too to Lee and Brendan and everyone else who contributed.

Contents

One

At The Post And Champing At The Bit p.1

Two

The Parade Ring - Runners And Riders:

Throwing The Towel In p.8

Well Bugger Me p.11

Don't Get Mad Get Steven p.16

When You've Gotta Go p.20

A Taxing Marriage p.23

Foo King Wan Car p.28

A Dead Cert p.31

Battle-Axe Brenda p.34

Trial And Error p.39

Nine Ten My Dad Likes Men p.47

A Cranberry Cretin p.49

In The Picture For Murder p.52

A Brick For A Prick p.55

Oggy Oggy Oggy p.57

Freshly Squeezed And Awestruck p.61

The Unsuspecting Mules p.65

I'd Kill For A Good Night's Sleep p.70

Awfully Funny p.74

My Dad's A Dick p.77

Swallowed Alive p.92

Peeved Parents p.96

Double The Heartache p.106

An Upside Down World p.110

Poppycock Or Not? p.115

Barbarism p.119

Ungrateful Little Bastard! p.124

Dropping Dad In It p.127

Tight Arsed Santa p.131

A Wee Map Of Africa p.133

The Gloved Hand p.136

Hanging Loose p.142

All That Glitters p.147

Tickled Pink p.151

Chop Chop We're Off To Bangkok p.159

Close Encounters Of The Turd Kind p.171

Snatch Of The Day p.184

Life's A Blast p.181

Three
The Winner's Enclosure

Jumping For Joy p.187

One

At The Post And Champing At The Bit

Around eighteen months ago a friend of mine, Graham, started to write a book, this one. But he never got to finish it because not long after he started it he died after being hit by a racehorse at Kempton Park.

He didn't really die after being hit by a horse at Kempton I just thought I'd put that for a laugh! Though no doubt if he'd have had the choice of how to go, because of his love for racing, being hit by a racehorse would probably have been his choice. (It'd have been far better than watching the poor bastard suffer the way did that's for sure. Just *when are they* going to find a cure for cancer?) Mind you, if he'd have still been alive when I started writing his book for him he'd have probably died from a heart attack when he read it and saw that I'd ballsed it up!

Graham wasn't a writer. And neither am I. As no doubt it'll show! But what Graham was, was a lover of horseracing. He was an apprentice jockey when he was in his teen's but he wasn't quite good enough and never got to fulfil his dream of becoming a professional jockey. But his passion for racing stayed with him. He loved it. He loved having a bet too. As do I. And I used to see Graham in the bookies most days. And like me and the other blokes in there he'd study the form, the trainer, the jockey etc. However *unlike* me and the other blokes Graham would also spend a lot of time looking at the horses names.

He was intrigued by the names of the horses and many a time he'd say to me, "I wonder why they called it that?" To which my reply usually was, "I've got no idea. And I don't fucking care as long as it wins!!" And he used to say - to anyone that'd listen, not that any of us did, we just used to tell him to shut up and let us concentrate on trying to pick the winners out for the day! - that behind the name of every horse there'd be a story. And one day he said to me, "I'm going to write a book." And when I asked him what it was going to be about he said that it was going to be about the names of racehorses and why owners have chosen the name they have. But about three months after he started it he was given the news that he had terminal cancer.

After Graham died I spoke to his wife about the book and I told her that if she wanted me to I'd try and finish the book for him and she said that Graham would've liked that and she thanked me for offering. Though if I knew then what I was letting myself in for I don't think I *would* have offered!

His wife said that his intention was to make it a *humorous* book and I presumed that Graham had done the bulk of it and that it'd be just a case of piecing everything together. But it turned out that Graham had only jotted ideas down and noted a few horses that had funny names, and that's about as far as he'd got. And due to his failing health he hadn't been able to take his research any further and contact any of the owners to get information about why they'd called their horse the name they had and what the story was behind it for doing so. And that's when I realised that I'd dropped a bollock by offering to do his book because it meant that I was going to have to do all of that!

Apart from not really having the time to write a complete book I really didn't fancy doing all the research that would obviously need doing. It'd have taken ages. So I came up with a different idea for the book. It wasn't quite what Graham intended I know, but it's turned out pretty good. Well I think it has anyway! And so too does Graham's wife who I ran the idea for it past first.

Graham's idea for his book was a good one but I don't think he realised just how difficult it would have been. First of all he would have needed to have found around forty or fifty horses that had funny names. He then would've had to have contacted all the owners, which would have been a task in itself trying to get contact details for them all, and ask them if they'd send him their story and hoped that they all replied. They might have done, they might not. I dare say that a few of them would have replied but I doubt very much that all of them would have done. Also, by basing the book purely on horses with funny names Graham was limiting himself somewhat - and missing out.

For every racehorse that has a *funny name* with a *funny story* behind it there are probably twenty 'intriguingly' named racehorses that have fascinating and extraordinary stories behind their names. That said, if you were to write a book about horses with intriguing names and the stories behind them you'd still have the same predicament as you would if writing a book about horses with funny names in that not all of the owners would get back to you with the information you wanted.

Another thought then crossed my mind.

As well as there being twenty or more intriguingly named horses with *intriguing* stories behind their names for every funnily named horse with a *funny* story behind its name there'll be a thousand people who *don't* own a racehorse who could name one after an event in their life and tell the story behind it if they *did* own one (if that makes sense!) be the story funny, intriguing, moving, inspiring, sad or bizarre. So to save time and effort, quite possibly *wasted* effort, contacting *real* racehorse owners for their stories I thought that a better idea would be to base the book on *would-be* racehorse owners who had interesting life-stories to tell.

So I set up a Facebook page called 'If I owned a racehorse' and I asked people to send me stories about things that have happened to them and think of a name for a horse that related to the story.

I also spoke with a few of Graham's mates one of whom was Billy and I asked him if he could help in any way. Billy's led a 'colourful' life and he said "Leave it with me." And Billy came up trumps! As did several others who I asked. Though I doubt very much that some of the horses names would be approved by the British Horseracing Authority!

I did end up doing a bit of research and I found out some pretty interesting things about the rules behind the naming of a racehorse that I never knew.

I knew that a name couldn't exceed eighteen characters, letters/numbers etc, the maximum allowed. But I didn't know that a horse's name couldn't end in "stud" "filly" "colt" "mare" or "stallion" or any other similar horse related terms. And I didn't know that a racehorse's name mustn't include the name of a real person or someone who has been dead for less than fifty years, unless written permission has been given by that person or by the family of the deceased. Nor did I know that names can't consist purely of numbers unless the number is above thirty and it's spelt out. For example you could name your horse "Sixty Nine" if you wanted to. Though that particular name/number may not be permitted as it could be deemed vulgar. So if you ever buy a racehorse and 69 is your favourite sexual position and you want to name it after it then you might have to think again! Doggy Fashion (*my* favourite position!) would probably also be banned. In actual fact it was, even though it was spelt differently. Though if spooning is your favourite sexual position you should be okay with that one!

On the subject of numbers, did you know that you can tell the sex of a horse by counting its teeth? Although it's far easier to just look underneath and see if there's a massive cock swinging around!

The reason that the name "Sixty Nine" may not be allowed is because a racehorse's name can't include suggestive, obscene or vulgar words and meanings and can't be in poor taste. And that's another reason why a lot of the horse's names given by people in this book wouldn't be allowed! And I was surprised to learn that around thirty percent of names submitted to the BHA are rejected because they're deemed too rude, although some are given the okay. And some names slip through the net after being 'disguised' slightly.

Some of the names that have been given the okay or that have slipped through are Hoof Hearted, Gee Spot, Fuchu, Slippery Dick, Thatz nackardit (that's knackered it) Effinmental (fucking mental) and Wear The Fox Hat (where the fuck's that.) Also given approval were Muff Diver, Little Knickers, Passing Wind OopsMyZipsDown, Foxy Fanny and Spank The Monkey! Two others that were given approval were Betty Swallocks and Mary Hinge (switch the first letters around of each of the names and you've got Sweaty Bollocks and Hairy Minge!) Surprisingly, 'Big Tits' was also approved. However some names were considered a bit *too rude*. These included Chit Hot, Hugh G Dildeaux (huge dildo) Ivor Hugh G Rection (I've a huge erection) Major B Oner, Pee Nesenvy, Norfolk Enchants (no fucking chance) Willy Be Hardigan (will he be hard again) Amavanna Threesome and Arfur Foulkesaycke (ah for fuck's sake.) Also banned were Ben Derhover and Ben Dimova. As were Cupid Stunt, MDick Hertz, (my dick hurts) Jack Schitt, Are Soles to You, Curl One Off and Choking The Chicken! Banned too was Oil Beef Hooked (say it in an Irish accent) which I amended slightly and used for the title of the book. I'm sure you don't need me to spell *that one* out for you. And I'll be fucked if I'm going too!

Apparently, out of devilment and for a bit of fun, a lot of racehorse owners give their horse a name in order to cause embarrassment for race commentators. And if the aforementioned horse names are anything to go by the owner's ploy is a good one! Imagine commentating on a race and as the horses race towards the finish line you've got to shout out, "Here comes Foxy Fanny, Ben Derhover Ivor Hugh G Rection. Well Oil Beef Hooked, Big Tits is alongside her. It looks like Amavanna Threesome! This is Chit Hot. Arfur Foulkesaycke, here comes Jack Schitt with a Major B Oner. Thatz nackardit!" And the Chinese named horse for one of the stories in the book definitely *would* cause embarrassment for any race commentator! Not that it'd be approved by the British Horseracing Authority in the first place! But hopefully this book meets *Graham's* approval. Rest In Peace mate. Though if there's a bar in heaven Graham's probably *resting pissed!*

*A male horse has forty two teeth by the way. And a massive cock!

Two

The Parade Ring - Runners And Riders

Horse name

Throwing The Towel In

Owner

Bob

Story behind the name

I work as an insurance broker selling life assurance. I work out of an office but I also visit people at their homes. I go to various types of areas in and around London ranging from the affluent wealthy parts to middle class areas to council estates. And one day I had an appointment on a council estate that was built of numerous blocks of flats, four or five of which were high rise ones.

The estate was in east London and it was like a maze walking through the different blocks trying to find the flat I was going to. I was dressed in a suit and tie and I looked slightly out of place and it must have been fairly obvious to the residents that I didn't live there. It was a little bit unnerving too as there were groups of youths hanging around in different parts of the estate and one or two had their hoods up, and it could have just been coincidence but whenever I walked past them one of them would take his phone out and call somebody as if they were letting them know a stranger was on their patch.

To be honest I couldn't wait to get out of there and as soon as I'd been to my appointment I did just that, though not without mishap.

The person I had the appointment with was very nice. He was married with a young daughter which was the reason he wanted to take out life assurance. He was quite witty too and he said that another reason he wanted life assurance was because he lived on that estate and he was taking his life into his own hands every time he left his flat.

I knew exactly how he felt!

He lived in one of the high rise blocks near the top floor and so when I left his flat I got the lift down to the ground floor, exited the block and began to walk back to my car and as I got to the middle of the block I felt a light 'thud' on my head. My first thoughts were that someone had dropped a brick on my head but then I realised that it couldn't have been a brick as the thud didn't feel that heavy and there was no pain.

Whatever it was was still on the top of my head so I put my hand on my head and I felt something that was about seven inches long and oblong in shape. It felt warm too, which I could feel because I've got a bald head. So I got hold of it and threw it and it landed against a wall that was about 6ft away. I then looked at my hand and saw that my palm and fingers were red. My initial thought was that it was a hot dog and that the red was Tomato Ketchup and as I was looking at my hand I heard this cackling laughter from above. I then heard a woman shout, "Have that you bald bastard!" And when I looked up, about fifteen floors up I saw two women leaning over their balcony howling with laughter. And when I looked towards the wall I realised that it wasn't a Hot Dog it was a sanitary towel that one of them had obviously just removed, which was why it felt warm, and dropped it on my head. I then also realised what the 'Tomato Ketchup' was; blood!

It absolutely disgusted me, it really did. I'd have rather they dropped a brick on my head like I first thought someone had than that. And when I told my wife about it she too was disgusted. But when I told my friends about it and colleagues at work they found it hysterical.

Why the two women decided to drop the sanitary towel on me personally I'll never know. It probably *wasn't* personal. They didn't know me so it could've just been that I was the unlucky one that happened to be passing at that time. Or maybe it was that they didn't like outsiders, it was obvious that I didn't live on the estate. Or they may have presumed I was working for the D.S.S. or that I was an undercover police officer or that I was a council official or some other similar authoritarian who isn't welcome there. Then again it could just have been that my bald head was a tempting target!

Horse name

Well Bugger Me

Owner

Vivienne

Story behind the name

'There's nowt as strange as folk' as the saying goes. And you certainly see some strange folk walking through the doors of A&E departments in hospitals.

I worked on reception at A&E for over ten years and you wouldn't believe some of the things I saw. Nor would you believe some of the excuses that some people gave for the 'accidents' they'd had.

One night this man came walking in. It was just gone 2am and as he was walking towards the desk I could see that he was walking awkwardly and that he looked like he was in some discomfort. I presumed he was going to say that he'd tripped and hurt his ankle but I nearly burst out laughing when he told me what was wrong with him, and I struggled to keep a straight face when he explained how it had happened. Or how he *said* it had happened.

He approached the desk rather sheepishly and when I asked him what the problem was he leant forward and quietly said, "I've got half a cucumber stuck up my anus." My colleague who was sat next to me heard what he'd said and she started tapping my foot with her foot which made me want to laugh even more. And after I'd asked him how it had got in there and he told me, she had to get up and go in the back because she could hardly contain herself.

He said that he liked to cook in the nude and that when he was preparing a salad to go with his meal he'd knocked the cucumber off the kitchen work top and as he'd gone to grab it he'd slipped on some cooking oil that he'd spilt on the tiled kitchen floor. He said that he managed to grab hold of the cucumber as it dropped but as he got hold of it his right leg slid forwards, and he said that as he slipped his hand with the cucumber in somehow went underneath him and between his legs. He said his left knee then buckled and gave way and he fell in a seated position and landed on his backside and because his hand with the cucumber in it was underneath him he landed on it and the cucumber went into his anus and the force of him landing caused it to snap in half! I don't know many people that cook entirely naked and I know even less people that cook entirely naked at two o'clock in the morning!

Believe it or not it's not uncommon for people to come into A&E with things stuck in their anus and that wasn't the only time that someone walked through the door with a cucumber stuck up their bum after buggering themselves with it. Another guy also came in one evening with one wedged in his rectum and his excuse for it being there just as ludicrous as the other man's excuse.

He was in his mid fifties and he said that he regularly used cucumber to get rid of the bags under his eyes, the black markings that people sometimes get as a result of tiredness and lack of sleep, though they're also common in older people due to ageing. People do use cucumber to help get rid of bags under their eyes though I don't think he'd been using one for that purpose!

He said that he'd taken the cucumber upstairs, cut two pieces off it, lay on the bed and closed his eyes and put the two pieces of cucumber over them. He said that he'd left the cucumber on the bed next to him and that he'd fallen asleep and was woken up by a sharp pain in his bottom. And he said that when he looked down he saw half of the cucumber lying between his legs on the bed and he could feel the other half stuck in his bum. And he said that he must have rolled over onto the cucumber in his sleep and it'd somehow gone into his backside, and when he turned back again it must have snapped in half!

Another guy gave an identical excuse when he came in with a vibrator stuck up his bum. He said that he'd got in bed not knowing that his wife had been using her vibrator and that she'd left it in the bed and he rolled onto in his sleep! And one Christmas a man came in with his penis stuck in a turkey! He was quite drunk, so he did have an excuse of sorts. He was with a few of his mates too. Who couldn't stop laughing!

He was a rugby player and it was his team's Christmas do and they'd all written 'dares' on pieces of paper and put them in a bowl and each player had to pick one out and do whatever the dare was. During the course of the night there'd been a raffle and a few of the prizes were turkeys and when this guy pulled out his dare it said, "Stuff the turkey."
Well you know what rugby players are like!

And so he did. But what he didn't realise was that his mates had put super glue all around the turkey's hole and squirted it inside it. And after he penetrated it a few times - and then walked around the room with his knob in it for a few minutes - he realised he couldn't get it off. And he turned up at A&E, with half of his team mates who were howling laughing, with the turkey stuck to his cock! And someone else once came in with a Cadburys Cream Egg stuck up his anus and the excuse he gave was that he'd eaten it whole without chewing it!

I also saw one or two men (it always seemed to be men!) come in with things stuck *to* them or *in* them that really shouldn't have been stuck where they were stuck who *didn't bother* making excuses as to what had happened, including one chap who walked in with his penis nailed to a plank of wood!

Some men have a fetish about inflicting pain on their own genitals. What joy they get out of it is beyond me, but, each to their own. He hadn't hammered the nail, or let someone else hammer a nail (apparently some men pay to have things like that done to them) through his cock, he'd stretched his foreskin over a piece of wood and driven a nail right through it! Just what pleasure would you get from doing such a thing?

If you're a guy reading this then you'll probably know how painful it can be when you get your pecker caught in your zip after you've been for a pee (my husband informs me it isn't pleasant!) so what the pain must be like when someone drives a six inch nail through your foreskin I dread to think! It must be excruciating.

Though perhaps the funniest, and strangest, sight I ever saw was when this guy came shuffling through the entrance of A&E with just a towel around his waist and a gag restraint in his mouth and with his hands handcuffed behind his back. And the reason he was shuffling was because he had metal shackles around his ankles, the kind you see chain gang prisoners in America wearing when they're working on a highway.

The gag restraint was leather and it had what looked like a red snooker ball in the middle of it which the fella had stuck in his mouth. It prevented him from speaking and he looked like he was in extreme pain and he kept motioning down towards his towel with his head whilst making painful muffling sounds. And when one of the nurses took him into the triage room and lifted up his towel she saw *just why* he was in such pain; he had a mousetrap clamped on his testicles!

She said his testicles were virtually black because of the lack of blood circulation getting to them caused by the mousetrap being clamped on them. She said his balls were right in the trap and the metal bar was embedded into them, and she said that judging by the severity of the bruising the mousetrap must have snapped shut on them!

I'm not sure what'd be worse for a man; hammering a nail through your foreskin or letting a mousetrap snap shut on your knackers! The mind really does boggle. They say you never know what goes on behind closed doors and a lot of extremely weird stuff certainly goes on behind the closed doors of some people's houses!

Though not everyone turns up at hospital when they've got an emergency or had an accident. Some people let you know *prior* that they may have an emergency - and that it will be the hospital's fault if they *do* have one.

Astonishingly, a woman once rang A&E on Christmas day asking how long she should cook the turkey for. The nurse who took the call told the woman that it wasn't an accident and emergency problem, to which the woman replied, "Well if we don't cook it properly we're going to get food poisoning and we'll all have to come in – then it *will* be your problem." Being ever helpful, like the NHS always are, the nurse told the woman to cook the turkey for thirty minutes per pound and it'll be fine. Hopefully it wasn't the same turkey that the rugby player had shagged on his Christmas do!

Horse name

Don't Get Mad Get Steven

Owner

Alan

Story behind the name

If there's one thing that really pisses me off it's standing in dog shit. I hate having to clean my shoes after I've stood in it as not only is it disgusting it's also a right pain in the arse trying to get it out of the grooves on the tread on the sole, which I usually end up doing with a lollipop stick. And I heave when I'm doing it. And the smell! Oh my god. It stinks.

And it's even worse if one of my kids stand in it because half the time they don't realise they've stood in it and they walk it right through the house. It's all down the hallway. It's in the kitchen. It's up the stairs. It's in their bedrooms. It gets everywhere.

Standing in dog shit REALLY annoys me. But there's something else about dog shit that annoys me even more than standing in it and that's dog owners who don't pick it up after their dog has done it and they just walk off leaving a pile of turd on the pavement. It really is inconsiderate. And not only is it inconsiderate it can also be dangerous because if dog shit gets into a kid's eyes it can cause them to go blind. It's rare but it can and has happened. But even if some dog owners who don't bother to pick their dog's shit up knew that, which I'm sure a lot do, the inconsiderate lazy bastards probably still wouldn't pick it up after them anyway.

There's a dog owner who lives near me who never picks his dog's crap up. I see him everyday taking his dog for a walk around the estate and not once has he bothered to pick his dog's shit up after it's had a crap. Even more annoying, on occasions, he's let his dog have a dump right outside my house.

I've often felt like going out and picking it up and throwing it at him or at least say something to him, the problem is he's got a right reputation and he's not the sort you'd want to get on the wrong side of. He's a nasty piece of work by all accounts and his dog looks a right nasty thing too. I've no idea what breed it is but it looks like it's some kind of cross between a Rottweiler and a Pit Pull. It's a horrible vicious looking thing that's always snarling and growling at people, just like its owner. I think he should be kept on a lead too. So although I've often felt like going out and saying something to him I never have as I don't really fancy getting beaten up off him or being attacked by his dog.

And not so long ago I pulled up outside my house one day and as I got out of my car what did I do? You guessed it, I stood in a pile of dog shit, and who do I see strolling up the road ahead, none other than Mr Nasty himself walking his snarling beast. And as annoyed as I was I didn't confront him. Call me a wimp if you want but I just didn't have the bottle. But as you often hear people saying, don't get mad get even.

There's also more than one way to skin a cat. Or dog as it was. Though more appropriately, a dog's owner.

So I got a piece of cardboard and a paper bag from out of the bin and I scraped the dog shit up off the pavement with the cardboard and put it in the bag. And over the next few days whenever I saw any dog shit I picked it up and put it in the paper bag and by the end of the week the bag was nearly full.

I knew where 'Thug Life' lived so I said to a couple of kids off the estate that if they went and posted the bag through his letter box I'd give them a tenner each and they said they would. They were about fourteen years old and one of them, Steven, was a 'bit of a rum un'. They laughed when I told them what was in it and why I wanted them to do it and they said that they didn't like the guy either because he was a bit of a bully.

So I gave them the bag and they said they'd do it later that night, and at around ten o'clock they came to my house and they were absolutely peeing themselves laughing. And when I asked them had they done it they said, "No, we did something better," and when I asked what it was they'd done they said, "We'll show you!" and one of them took out his phone.

He'd videoed his mate going up to the blokes front door but instead of posting the paper bag through his letter box he put it on his doorstep. He then took out a cigarette lighter and set fire to the bag and knocked on the door and ran off and they both hid behind a car opposite his house. The bloke opened the door, saw the paper bag on fire on his doorstep and out of instinct began stepping on it to put it out. He then kicked it off the step, and after he'd looked downwards you heard him shout, "You fucking dirty little bastards!" as he realised he had dog shit all over his foot. He also had it all the way up his leg and inbetween his toes too because he'd answered the door with just a towel around him and nothing else! He must have either just got out of the shower or was getting into it when he heard the knock on the door and came down and answered it.

It couldn't have worked out any better and even though he still lets his dog shit anywhere it pleases and he still doesn't pick it up afterwards I can live with it because I'm happy that I've got my own back on him for repeatedly having his dog's shit all over my shoes. I'm just extra careful when I step out of my car! And no doubt Mr Nasty is extra careful when he opens his front door now when someone knocks on, and he probably puts a pair of wellies on first before he opens it.

Horse name

When You've Gotta Go

Owner

Martin

Story behind the name

My wife and I were looking to book a last minute holiday for the two of us and our six month old baby son and we found a really cheap one to Benidorm. I'd never been to Benidorm before and I never really fancied it to be honest as I'd heard stories about it being full of hen and stag parties and the like and I didn't think it was really the place to go for a family holiday. I'd also seen the television series 'Benidorm' and even though I found it funny it did put me off going there a little bit. But after reading the reviews on Tripadvisor about the hotel we'd found and the majority of them saying that it was ideal for families, and on the hotel's website it said that it was a family orientated hotel and that it didn't allow hen and stag parties or groups of rowdy youths, we went ahead and booked it.

We had a night flight which arrived in Alicante at midnight and by the time we'd gone through arrivals and got our bags and boarded the coach to transfer to the hotel it was about 1am. When we got on the coach there were a small group of lads on it already. They'd been drinking throughout the flight and they were a little bit loud and they were swearing a bit, but we half expected things like that, though to be fair to them they did curb their language when they saw we had a baby with us. Not that our son could understand the language they were using but at least they showed a bit of respect which was nice to see.

There was also a large group of women on the coach, around twenty of them, and who were about the same age as me and my wife, late thirties, early forties. They were considerably more drunk than the group of lads. They were completely pissed actually. And they were a lot louder too. They made the group of lads seem like choir boys in comparison.

They were shouting and singing and swearing, and one or two of them were lifting their tops up and flashing their breasts. The group of lads thought it was brilliant, and I kept getting told off by my wife for looking! But it was a bit much to be honest and some of the older people on board weren't impressed at all. But seeing as how we only had to put up with it for another three quarters of an hour until we got to our hotel it wasn't that much of a big deal for us. We were just grateful that they wouldn't be staying in the same hotel as us.

They were sat at the back of the coach and we were sat half way down and about twenty minutes into the journey one of the women came up to us and asked us if we had a spare nappy that she could have. I didn't think anything of it at first and said yes and my wife got one out of our baby's travel bag and gave it to her. She said thanks and then walked back up the aisle to the back of the coach where she was sat with her friends.

It's splitting hairs but in actual fact she *slurred* 'thanks' as opposed to saying it and she *staggered* back up the aisle as opposed to walking, but at least it'll give you an idea of how drunk they all were.

It suddenly dawned on me that none of the women had babies with them so I said to my wife how I thought it was a bit odd why she would want a nappy if none of them had babies in tow. My wife said that she thought it was a bit odd as well and just as she said it we heard howls of laughter and cries of "You dirty bitch" coming from the back of the coach. So we turned around and looked back. And when we did we saw the woman who'd asked for the nappy standing up in the middle of the aisle with her knees slightly bent and with her skirt hitched up to her waist and with her knickers around her ankles. And she was holding the nappy between her legs pissing into it! She could hardly stand up and there was as much of it running down her legs as there was actually going into the nappy. And there was a big pool of it starting to gather around her bare feet. Then when she'd finished she just flung the nappy under the seat, pulled her knickers up and sat back down and carried on drinking. When you've got to go you've got to go. But not in the aisle of a packed coach!

Before we went we'd heard numerous stories of the kinds of things to expect in Benidorm but we certainly weren't expecting that. It was disgusting but funny at the same time, though not many others on the coach, apart from the group of lads, were laughing. I've never seen anything like it. I think even the producers of the television series Benidorm would struggle to come up with a scene like that! Though if they ever re-enacted it for one of the episodes I'm sure it would go down very well with fans of the show. And even though our hotel was fine and all in all we had a good time, it was our first, and last time, we ever went on holiday to Benidorm.

Horse name

A Taxing Marriage

Owner

Ronnie

Story behind the name

The first part of this story may be of interest, and quite helpful, to anyone who is self employed in the building trade and who does a lot of cash jobs but doesn't declare them to the tax man, like most builders do. Or should that be like most builders don't! And the second part may be of interest if you happen to be in the process of going through a divorce or separation and you don't want your other half to get her hands on your hard earned dosh. And if like me you happen to be a builder who doesn't declare all of his cash jobs to the tax man *as well as* going through a separation, like I was at the time, then there's a lesson here for you to be learned. And no doubt you'll laugh at my expense at the latter part of it when you read it. Just like all my friends did when I told them about it.

I'm a window fitter by trade and at the time I was working for a company on a self employed basis and every week they'd pay my wages into my bank account. I also used to do a lot of 'foreigners', cash jobs outside of work if you're not familiar with the term, and this money I *didn't* pay into my bank account because I didn't want the Inland Revenue to know about it because if they did I would've had to have paid the tax on it. So I just used the money from my foreigners to live on and hardly ever withdrew cash from the bank from my wages and just left it in my account to cover direct debits for bills and so on.

Me and my wife weren't getting on at the time and our marriage was deteriorating and a divorce was on the cards. I hated the cow, and she hated me, and we more or less led separate lives. We didn't have any kids and so what was hers was hers and what was mine was mine, though the bank account was a joint account and both her and my wages went into it. This was another reason I didn't want to pay the cash from my foreigners into it. So not only did I have to hide it from the tax man I also had to hide it from my wife because I didn't want her getting half of it when we divorced. So I had to think of a good place to hide it in the house. Somewhere that not only would it be safe from *her* finding it but also safe from any burglars that might break in and find it. Though if it was a choice between the two I'd rather a burglar have it!

I found the perfect place to hide it that neither she nor any burglar would ever dream of looking. And little did my wife know that when she was asleep at night and she was having a dream herself my money was only about two inches away from her head. That's because I'd hidden it in the headboard.

It was the perfect place to hide it because it was an aluminium headboard that had poles at either side of it that were about 4ft long and they had a fancy metal cap on the top of them that unscrewed with an Allen key. So every time I earned cash from my foreigners, which was usually a few hundred quid at a time, I rolled it up, unscrewed the cap, pushed it inside, screwed the cap back on and hid the key.

The headboard was a right ugly old thing (a bit like my wife) and I never really liked it from the first day she bought it. I never really liked my wife either from the first day I married her but we all make mistakes! But the headboard ended up coming in very handy as my wife would never have thought that I'd be hiding money in it. And burglars wouldn't think of looking in it either let alone pinching it if they broke in. They may have ran off with the tele or the DVD player but the headboard was probably the last thing burglars would run away with. Thinking about it, the headboard would've been the *second* last thing in our house that burglars would have wanted to run away with. *My wife* would have been the last thing that a burglar - or any other bloke for that matter - would want to run away with. They'd have taken one look at her and just ran off. Though strangely, in the end someone did run off her. I still can't fathom that one out.

A couple of months later I received a letter from HMRC saying that they wanted to speak to me regarding undeclared earnings. I was dreading it to be honest and anyone that has been investigated by the tax man will know what a nightmare it is. They look into everything, and I do mean EVERYTHING. Including asking things like how often do you go out socialising. How many pints do you have when you go to the pub. Do you follow football, if so, how often do you go. Have you got a season ticket. How often do you go away on holiday. How often do you and your wife go out for a meal (that one was easy, never.) How much do you spend on clothes. How much is your monthly mortgage payment, or your rent. How much is your gas, water and electric, they ask you all sorts.

Basically it's about income and expenditure and if your expenditure is more than your income then they want to know where the extra money is coming from that pays for it all. And my downfall was when they looked at my bank statements, which you have to provide. Because when they looked at them they saw that I hardly ever touched my wages and they wanted to know how if I wasn't using my wages to live on then what money *was* I using. They obviously knew I was earning money from doing foreigners and not declaring it. How they knew I'll never know, but they did. And this is the first lesson for any self employed builders.

Even if you're doing cash jobs that you're not declaring still take money out of your bank account regardless if you spend it or not. Do it every Friday, say £200. Because that way you can justify where the money came from to go to the pub or go to the football or go for a meal or take your kids out for the day. It's even more important to do it if you've got kids actually because you'll be spending a lot more money and if you can't show where that money has come from they'll have you. And that's what happened to me.

Obviously I didn't unscrew the caps off the headboard and take the money out, which was well over £5,000, and give it to them and say, "This is what I've earned." I just said that I do one or two foreigners every now and then, which they didn't really believe, and they estimated that the tax I owed was £1,200, which wasn't far off actually, and which I agreed to pay back out of my wages every month. I also left the foreigners alone for a while just in case they were watching me. But at least I still had over six grand hidden in the headboard. Or so I thought. As it panned out I didn't even end up with a headboard let alone one with six grand hidden inside it. And that's because after a blazing row with my wife one night which culminated in me shouting at her, "Why don't you just take what's yours and fuck off." The following day I came home from work to find she'd done just that and taken the headboard with her, and the next time I heard from her it was via her solicitor. Then six months later we were divorced and I never saw her, or the headboard with my hard earned dosh inside it, ever again. And as much as I was frustrated knowing that I'd never see my money again, I was equally elated knowing that I'd never clap eyes on my wife again either.

And there's lesson two for you. If you're hiding money from your wife never hide it in the headboard because even though burglars might not run off with it your wife just might. And if by chance you happen to be shacked up with my ex-wife you may want to get yourself a 2.4mm allen key and unscrew the caps on that hideous looking headboard you've got attached to your bed, you're welcome to what's inside it. You're also welcome to that hideous looking thing that sleeps on the bed next to you with her head against it.

Horse name

Foo King Wan Car

Owner

Peter

Story behind the name

Have you ever heard of Gaelic Prawns? I hadn't either. Neither had I heard of Swat and Sore Pock (Sweet and Sour Pork) or Pecking Stalled Craspy Checkin (Peking Style Crispy Chicken) until me and a couple of mates went in this Chinese restaurant in Santa Ponsa in Majorca a few years ago.

It was late on, gone midnight, and me Mark and Steve were the only ones in the restaurant. I think it was about to close when we turned up but they let us in anyway. It was only a small place, a family run type thing, and the woman came over and gave us a menu each and we ordered some beers and then we looked at the menu. And as we started reading it we saw that it was full of spelling mistakes. Nearly everything was spelt wrong. Most of the dishes had a letter missing or the wrong letter had been used in the words so instead of it saying *Beef* curry it said *Bef* curry and instead of *Garlic* prawns it said *Gaelic* prawns and instead of it saying *Fried* rice it said *Fred* rice. And it had things like spring *rules*, and Satan checkin, which presumably was Satay chicken, and fred moshrooms in ooster sauce and *barbie*cued spared *rips*. Inadvertently they'd even named a dish after Eric Cantona and instead of it saying Cantonese Style Roast Duck it said Cantona Stalled Rost Dock! It looked like a kid had written it and it turned out that one had.

We set off laughing at all the mistakes and you know what it's like when you're pissed you laugh even more at the silliest things. What made it worse, or *better* looking back, was that Mark has got a really raucous laugh. He's got one of those infectious laughs that makes others laugh even more, and the woman, who was stood watching from the counter and who probably wasn't overjoyed in the first place that three drunks had come in just as she was about to close, came over. She must have realised what we were laughing at, and in an abrupt tone, and not in the best of English, shouted, "Why you laugh at my menu?" One of us, I forget who, apologised and gave some excuse that we weren't laughing at the menu and that we were laughing at something else but she knew we were laughing at it. I bet we weren't the first ones to laugh at it either. No doubt every fucker that went in there pissed themselves when they read it! So we tried our best to contain ourselves and not to laugh, but again, you know what it's like when you're pissed and you've got the giggles, once you start it's hard to stop.

She was starting to get the hump and in an even more abrupt tone, and in a loud voice, she said, "You want order or not?" So inbetween bouts of laughter we said yes.

She really was getting annoyed and she more or less shouted, "WHAT YOU WANT?" So trying not to laugh Steve and Mark ordered theirs. She then looked at me and barked, "WHAT 'BOUT YOU?" And so with putting emphasis on the spelling errors I said, "I'll have the GAELIC Prawns and two spring RULES to start, and I'll have SATAN'S CHECKIN in OOSTER sauce and can you ask FRED if I can have some of his rice," and then I said, "Oh, and do the BARBIE-cued spare ribs come with a doll?"

That was the final straw for her! And in her broken English come Chinese accent she screamed, "It's no funny! It's no funny! Don't make fun. My Son write menu. He only ten year old. He half Chinese half Spanish and cannot read or write plopply." And Steve picked the menu up, held it in his hand and looked at me and Mark and said, "That's handy 'innit. A Chinese menu written in English by a ten year old mixed race dyslexic Spaniard - no fucking wonder it's full of mistakes!" He then closed the menu, put it on the table and said to the woman, "Just do me egg and chips, it'll be easier."

Well I started howling laughing. And I couldn't stop! I had tears streaming down my face and I nearly fell off my chair I was laughing that much, which made the woman even more annoyed than she already was! And she screamed, "You Fooking Wanka! Stop laughing." Well that was it. It was the final straw for *me*! I was nearly choking laughing. And in the end I had to get up and walk out because I was laughing that much. And as I was walking towards the door the woman shouted, "Come back. Where you go? You ordered food." So I said, "I've changed my mind - I'm going for a DOOOONER KEBAPPA instead!"

Horse name

A Dead Cert

Owner

Sharon

Story behind the name

When I was young I used to love going to my grandparents house and whenever we went my Grandpa would always tell me funny stories about things he's seen and done. Looking back, his stories were a bit over the top and slightly exaggerated to say the least, if true at all. And as he was telling me them my Grandma would usually give a little shake of her head and smile and say to me, "Don't believe him!" because more often than not his stories *weren't* true and he was just making them up, like Grandpa's do.

But one of the stories he told me always stuck in my mind and for once one of his stories was actually true and as I've got older I've since read about it numerous times. It's one of the most amazing stories I've ever read and it's about a friend of my Grandpa's called Frank Hayes who was a jockey and my Grandpa went to see him race at Belmont Park race track in 1923.

His friend had never won a race before, in fact it was only his second race and he didn't have much chance of winning that day either as the horse he was riding, 'Sweet Kiss' was a 20/1 outsider. But despite the odds it won. But my Grandpa's friend, Frank, didn't get to celebrate his first win. He didn't even get to see himself pass the winning post let alone get to celebrate his first win and that's because he was dead when he passed it.

He'd suffered a heart attack mid race and slumped forward on the horse but miraculously he stayed on it and it raced home to win. At first when people went over to congratulate him they thought he was just leaning over the horse saying 'well done' to it in its ear. But my Grandpa, who was watching from the side of the racecourse, said that when his friend still remained slumped forwards in the saddle as people were gathering around him he realised something was wrong. It later transpired that he'd suffered heart failure just after he'd taken the lead.

My Grandpa said that no-one knew for sure what caused his friend to have a heart attack and that it came as a total shock to everyone because he was fit and healthy. Though it was reported in some newspapers that the likely cause was down to the strenuous training he'd been doing in order to make the weight which put too much strain on his heart. He'd apparently lost a stone in a matter of days. Other reports suggested that it could have been caused by the excitement of him knowing that he had the chance to win his first race as he took the lead and it brought on a huge adrenaline rush which caused his heart to race too much, which in turn brought on the heart attack. But whatever it was that caused it, it was very sad.

It was sad for the horse too because even though it won it never raced again. Not because it was too old, it was because other jockeys declined to ride it, possibly because of superstition thinking they might suffer the same fate as Frank Hayes. It also acquired a new name and instead of it being called by its *proper* name 'Sweet Kiss', people nicknamed it 'Sweet Kiss Of Death.'

As the race was won in very unusual circumstances and because the stewards weren't quite sure what the rules were under such circumstances and didn't know what to do, the rules were waived and Frank Hayes was declared the official winner. Thus, the ruling made him the only jockey ever to win a race whilst deceased. It's also the only time in sporting history where a competition has been won by a dead person. Ironically, before the race began Frank Hayes said to his fellow jockeys, "It's a good day for making history."

He did just that.

So the next time your grandpa is telling you a story and your grandma smiles at you and says, 'don't believe him,' she may not always be right because some of his stories may well be true.

Horse name

Battle-Axe Brenda

Owner

Linda

Story behind the name

I was born and raised in the Lake District and many, many years ago when I was at college I had a summer job working for a boat hire company on Lake Windermere. They used to hire out rowing boats to tourists and my job was to take the tickets people had bought at the kiosk and help them in and out of the boats and make sure they were all given the life jackets that they had to wear.

As well as tourists, locals used to hire the boats too and there was one couple who used to come every week. They were an older couple who were retired. The husband was a lovely man and he always smiled and said hello. He was always very pleasant and polite and he came across as being very mild mannered, meek even. We never knew his name, though we nicknamed him 'Likeable Larry' and whenever he came he'd always have a chat with us - when he was allowed too. That's because his wife 'Battle-Axe Brenda' as we nicknamed *her* was a right old bag and she was forever nagging at him and telling him to hurry up and to get a move on and to 'shape yourself will you.'

She really was an old hag and she was really domineering and bossy and it was obvious that she was the one who wore the pants in their house and that he was a downtrodden henpecked husband who'd do what he was told just to have a quiet life. Sometimes he'd see me watching them walking towards me and he'd give me a look as though to say 'have you heard her going on' as his wife nagged away, and I'd give him a kind of sympathetic knowing smile in return. And one day he said something funny to my boss that made me laugh.

As he came walking down the jetty, with his wife about twenty yards behind him going on with herself as usual, my boss said to him, "Two life vests?" and he quietly replied, "Just the one will do today, one of us might not be coming back," implying his wife might drown! And he half smiled as if to say 'if only' and nodded towards his wife who was storming up the jetty with a face like thunder barking her orders at him to get in the boat.

They used to have their lunch out on the lake and they'd bring a small wicker type picnic basket with them which had sandwiches in it and a flask of tea and other bits. And they'd hire a rowing boat and he'd row it out into the middle of the lake and they'd spend an hour out there having their lunch.

They usually came on a Wednesday and one Wednesday I saw 'Larry' walking over to the kiosk to get his ticket. He had his picnic basket with him but he was alone and his wife wasn't with him. He came up the jetty and he gave me his ticket and I asked him if his wife was coming along and he said that she wouldn't be. And he said that she was at home as she'd fallen and hurt her ankle and couldn't get about. I was tempted to say that I bet he was glad so he could have a bit of piece of quiet but I resisted, even though he'd have probably agreed. And he got in the rowing boat and he rowed out into the middle of the lake as usual.

A little while later one of the other boats came back in. A family had been out in it and as they got out of it and on to the jetty the dad said that he'd seen something that looked a bit odd. And when I asked what, he said that he'd seen someone in one of the rowing boats open what looked like a box and take something out of it that was wrapped in black plastic and drop it in the water and it sank. So I asked which boat it was and he pointed to it. It was Larry's. So I said I'd ask the person when they got back.

When Larry came in I helped him out of the boat. He said thanks like he always did and then said, "I enjoyed that. It was nice out there on my own. I might do it again tomorrow." I commented that he may as well while the weather was nice but I never mentioned anything about him dropping stuff in the water, and the following day he turned up again like he'd said he would.

We had some binoculars in the kiosk that we used mainly for safety reasons to check on people every so often when they were out on the lake to make sure they were okay. So I got them and watched Larry. And when he was near the middle of the lake he opened his picnic basket and took something out of it. It was about eighteen inches long and looked fairly thick. Whatever it was, was wrapped in what looked like a black bin liner, and he dropped it in the water and it sank. And when his hour was nearly up he started heading back in, and like I didn't do the previous day, when he got out of the boat I never mentioned it to him about dropping something in the water. I didn't mention it to anybody else either, including my boss. Although some time later I did mention it to a few of my friends at college.

Two days later he came back again and did the same thing. And all in all over a three week period he came six times. And he did exactly the same thing every time; went out on a boat, took a parcel out of his picnic basket that was wrapped in black plastic and dropped it in the water in the middle of the lake.

Then all of a sudden he stopped coming and I never saw him or his wife ever again. That's when I began to think he'd done something to his wife.

The penultimate time I saw him I asked him how his wife was doing and he said that her ankle was getting better. But he seemed more bubbly and jolly. He was always pleasant and smiley but over that three week period he seemed even more happier and cheerful than he normally was. It was like a weight had been lifted off his shoulders and I thought has he got to the end of his tether with her nagging at him all the time and bossing him around and he's finally snapped and killed her and chopped her up and got rid of her body in the lake? Then I thought no, that's a ridiculous thing to think. He wouldn't do that, surely? But the more I thought about it the more I began to think he had done. Even now I think he did.

At the time - as I sometimes think now - I thought that if he'd cut her legs and arms off, there's four parts, which he could fold in half at the knee and elbow and they'd easily fit into his picnic basket. That would just leave her head and upper body. If he then chopped her head off that's *another* two parts, her head and the trunk of her body, which equalled six parts and which was the same amount of times he came and dropped a parcel in the lake.

When it first crossed my mind that he might have done it I even measured the top part of my own body from my hips to my collar bone and it was just under 2ft. And his wife wasn't the biggest of women either so her trunk would have easily fitted into the picnic basket, as would her head.

It may well have just been my imagination running wild but it seemed highly coincidental. Then around a year later rumours began circulating that the body of a woman had been found in the lake. My heart stopped for a moment when I heard about it but it was later reported on the news that the body had been found in Lake Coniston, not Windermere. There have also been reports of the bodies of people who have been murdered being found in lakes elsewhere, and one I read about had the head and hands missing. So it does happen.

Even now I often wonder if I should have said something and perhaps if there were reports of a woman going missing in the area I may well have done. But there wasn't, so I never did. Though even if 'Likeable Larry' *had* finally snapped and murdered his wife and dumped her in the lake I'm sure those who knew him would have had sympathy for him as it must have been torment for him living with Battle-Axe Brenda.

Horse name

Trial And Error

Owner

An acquaintance of Billy's

Story behind the name

I've no idea who it was that came up with the phrase 'crime doesn't pay' but whoever it was certainly wasn't a criminal because as all criminals know crime *does* pay and it can pay very handsomely.

A better saying would be 'crime is all about trial and error' because if you make an error whilst committing crime chances are you'll end up on trial for it and if found guilty you'll be punished by the courts. But some people who commit crime or who are heavily involved in it not only make errors, they make errors of judgement. And sometimes the consequences of making an error of judgement can be far worse than the consequences of just making an error, and in some cases it's not the courts who punish them for it. It's people like me.

'Enforcer' 'Hired Muscle' 'Henchman', there are various terms for people like myself. And unlike in the courts, in the world I operate in there are no guidelines or rules as regards to the type of punishment handed out. It's whatever the person who is paying sees fit, and the following will give you an idea of the kinds of things that can happen if you're involved in criminality and you cross the wrong people.

This one didn't directly involve me I just happened to be there discussing another 'job' and I saw the end result. I was with somebody in their office one day and as we were speaking his secretary came in and said that someone was here to see him. So he said excuse me and got up and left the room. I could see him speaking to this person through the door and when they'd finished talking he came back in. He sat down behind his desk and opened one of the draws and he took out a small jewellery type gift box and pushed it across his desk to me and said, "Take a look at that." So I opened it. And inside was a silver necklace and it had a pendant on it and dangling from the pendant was a finger. It was the little finger, and it had been cut off someone's hand, and the hand belonged to the fella who he'd just been talking too. And as I looked at it he said, "I don't know what to do with that. Keep it to show people so they'll know what lengths I'll go to, or give it back to him as a reminder not to fuck with me ever again."

The finger wasn't in its entirety by the way, as in with the nail and skin still on it. It was just the bone. It'd been completely stripped of all the skin and tissue and then it had been cleansed and mounted on the pendant. Where and who it'd been taken too to have it done I have no idea though I doubt very much he'd have got it done at Beaverbrooks or Pandora.

I suspect that it might have been quite painful for that fella having his finger cut off but it probably wasn't half as painful as what happened to the person whom I was there to discuss. I'm not going to divulge the reasons why this occurred, let's just say that in the eyes of the person who asked for this to be carried out they thought the person on the receiving end of it warranted such punishment. And his punishment was to have his legs broken.

The person who was to have his legs broken had actually been given an option, not by me I might add. And his options were either to have his legs broken or be kneecapped by being shot in both knees, and he chose to have his legs broken. So we broke them.

We took him to a lock up garage - without a struggle, he went willingly - and we sat him on a chair. He put both feet up on another chair opposite and we asked him if he was ready. He said he was, so two of us picked up a concrete lintel that we'd had put there and dropped it onto his shins halfway between his knees and his ankles. The pain must have been immense. He screamed the place down, and afterwards, as instructed by the person who'd asked me to carry the job out, I arranged for him to be taken to hospital.

A few days later the person who'd asked for it to be done went to visit him in hospital. I don't know if he took him a bunch of grapes and a bottle of Lucozade but he visited him all the same. He asked him how he was doing and the guy said that it wasn't as bad as it could have been as his legs weren't actually broken and that they were just partially fractured, which was surprising considering the amount of pain he was in. And so my 'employer' said to him, "They're not broken? Well in that case I'm going to have to do them again then aren't I."

The guy thought he was joking, but he wasn't. And my employer reminded him of the deal which was that he was either kneecapped or he had both of his legs broken, and seeing as how his legs weren't broken the deal wasn't complete, therefore he'd have to have them done again.

Ruthless, maybe, but a deal's a deal, and so after spending the next ten weeks in traction, when he came out we broke them again. And this time they *did* break - in half.

We used the same lintel that we'd used before and we dropped it in the exact same place on his shins as we did the first time. We did more than drop it actually. We *slammed* it down, just to make sure. And because they'd already been partially fractured his legs just snapped. They were literally dangling by the skin and you could see the bone sticking out. Job done.

Sometimes though just the *threat* of violence is enough to achieve results and there's no need to cut fingers off or snap people's legs in half. I also sometimes give people an 'out', an opportunity for them to settle up, or whatever, whilst at the same time leading them to believe that they've done okay out of it and that they've got off lightly. Here's an example.

I was once asked to get £50,000 back off someone, of which I was getting half. Taking half may seem a lot, and it's an old cliché, but fifty percent of something is better than a hundred percent of nothing.

It was a business deal, a legit one supposedly, and this geezer had taken this other guy's money but instead of investing it as he should have done he just fucked off with it. So the guy who's money it was asked me to get it back. It then became apparent that it wasn't the first time this person had taken money off people and not done what he should have with it. And because things were getting a bit hot for him he upped sticks and went to Canada and when he was there he opened a steak house with the money he'd conned out of people. But his *mis*take was thinking he couldn't be found. But the world's a small place these days and you can be on the other side of the world in Australia or New

Zealand in less than 24 hours. And you can be in Canada in less than eight. So me and a friend of mine paid him a visit.

We booked a table in his restaurant and as luck would have it, it was him that came over and served us and when he asked us what we'd like I said, "We'll have the 8oz sirloin with chips and two bottles of Bud please." He said okay and said that someone would bring the drinks over and that the steaks would be about twenty minutes, so I said that'd be fine. And as he turned to walk away I said, "Oh, and Michael, I'd also like that seventy five grand you owe Anthony."

He looked like he'd seen a ghost. He completely shit himself and the first thing he said was, "I don't owe him seventy five grand, I only owe him fifty." Straight away I had him. He'd admitted he owed it. So now was the time to put pressure on him.

I told him that the other £25,000 was interest that Anthony had added to it. He hadn't added it to it, I just said that. I also told him that I'd been instructed by Anthony to give him a good hiding. Again, I hadn't, I'd made that up too. Now he really *was* panicking because going through his mind he was thinking that not only did he have to pay the fifty thousand back that he'd took, he was also going to have to pay a further £25k on top. PLUS he was going to get a right pasting.

I could tell by looking at his face that he was about to fill his pants. He was getting in a right state, which was how I wanted him to be. So I said to him, "I'll tell you what. If you agree to pay the £50,000 you owe I'll ring Anthony and ask him will he accept it and forget about the other £25,000. Also, if you pay it - and you don't fuck me about - I won't give you a good hiding." He agreed. And he paid it within a week.

So sometimes, instead of violence, by using mind games that leads people to believe that they've done alright out of the deal, everybody's happy. Here, Anthony was happy because he got half of his money back. I was happy because I got paid £25k, and Michael was happy because he thought he'd got away with not having to pay an extra twenty five thousand and he'd avoided getting a good hiding.

And here's a tip for you to finish off with.

Be very careful what you say and who you say it in front of because it doesn't matter where you are you never know who might be listening.

I was at Barcelona airport once returning home from something I was doing in Spain for somebody and I was sat with my back to this guy who was on his phone. I wasn't ear wigging but I couldn't help but here what he was saying.

He was discussing a 'business deal' part of which was to do with a large property development in South Africa and I heard a certain person's name mentioned. I knew of this person and he was at the top of the tree in our world and from what this guy was saying he was quite obviously dropping his name to whoever it was he was speaking to in order to sway the deal more in his favour.

Dropping names, when you haven't been given permission to do so by the person whose name you're dropping, can land you in hot water. It's not something you do and you're either very brave or very fucking stupid if you do it.

So I got up and walked about ten yards in front of him and stood as though I was using my phone and as he was busy talking I took a photo of him and when I got back home I went to see the person whose name he'd dropped. I told him where I'd seen this guy and what I'd heard him say and said that I thought it may be of interest to him and showed him the photo I'd took. He said that he knew this person but that he had no connection to the deal or to the development. He asked me to send the picture to him on his phone, which I did, and I left it with him. He then did a bit of digging and he found out that the guy at Barcelona airport had used his name in order to get the better part of a multi-million pound deal from which he stood to make half a million. But he didn't contact him or say anything to him. Instead, he left it for over three years until the project was finished and everyone had been paid out. He then rang the guy up and asked him how he was doing and said that he hadn't spoken to him in a while and asked how things were. He said that he hoped all was well and what have you, and made small talk with him. He then mentioned that he'd heard about the project in South Africa and that it was all finished and the guy said that was right and that he'd done very nicely out of it. So he said to him, "Yes, I believe so. And I believe you owe me £250,000."

The guy asked why would he owe him £250k when he had nothing to do with it and he hadn't put any money into it. So he explained about me over hearing him dropping his name at Barcelona airport three years previously and sent him the picture I took. He then told him that he'd spoken to other parties involved in the deal and they said that the reason he'd got such a big chunk was because he'd told them he had his backing, when in fact, he hadn't. He then pointed out to him that if it wasn't for him using his name he wouldn't have got such a big chunk - if any involvement at all in the deal - therefore he was entitled to half. The guy then had no alternative but to pay up because he knew what would have happened if he hadn't. This was one person you definitely wouldn't want on your case and having a finger cut off or a leg broken would be like having a slap on the wrist in comparison to what might have happened to the fella had he chosen not to pay.

Horse name

Nine Ten My Dad Likes Men

Owner

Lee

Story behind the name

When my daughter was in primary school she wrote a poem that had the teachers in tears - tears of laughter. It also left me with a little bit of explaining to do.

She was five at the time and when I went to pick her up from school, when I was waiting in the playground and the kids came out her teacher came walking over to me with a piece of paper in her hand. She also had a smile on her face. I noticed the other teachers were looking over at me as well and they too were smiling and grinning. Ella, my daughter, came running over to me as usual and wrapped her arms around me and gave me a hug and then ran off and played with her friends. Her teacher then told me that the kids had all been asked to write a poem that day and that the one Ella had written had them in stitches laughing and she said she thought that I might want to see it and she handed it to me. This is Ella's poem:

One –Two, Buckle My Shoe
Three – Four, Knock On The Door
Five – Six, The Dog Plays Tricks
Seven – Eight, Close The Gate
Nine –Ten, My Dad Likes Men!

I nearly fell over in the playground doubled up laughing. No wonder the teachers were all grinning and smirking at me! I then found myself trying to explain to Ella's teacher that I wasn't that way inclined and that I didn't fancy other men and that I didn't have homosexual tendencies. I've still got the piece of paper with the poem written on it and it still makes me laugh whenever I read it. Ella had obviously written it based on the original 'buckle my shoe' nursery rhyme and for her first attempt at writing poetry it wasn't a bad effort, even though it was somewhat inaccurate!

Horse name

A Cranberry Cretin

Owner

Anne

Story behind the name

You may have heard the old joke about a woman who applies for a job in a lemon grove and the boss asks her if she has any experience in picking lemons and the woman replies, "Yes, I have. I picked one thirty years ago and I've been married to him ever since." Well if I were ever to apply for a job in a lemon grove and the boss asked *me* that question that would be my answer as well because my husband must be the biggest lemon there is.

I once had cystitis and as most women know cranberry juice can help relieve the pain and soothe the stinging feeling, so I asked my husband if he'd go to the shop and get some for me and told him what it was for. He said he would and off he went, and when he came back he handed me a carrier bag with it in. So I got a glass and took the bottle of cranberry juice out of the bag and as I took it out I saw a packet of cotton wool in there too that he'd also bought. So I asked him what it was for and he looked at me with a slightly bemused look on his face as though I was asking him a stupid question and he replied, "To dab it on with." So I said, "Dab it on with? What are you on about? Dab what on where?" And he said, "To dab the cranberry juice on with." The idiot thought that I was going to dab the cranberry juice on my vagina and so he bought the cotton wool to do it with!

I collapsed on the sofa in a fit of laughter and as I was holding my sides to prevent them from splitting he said, "What's so funny?" And so I said, "The cranberry juice is for drinking you imbecile not for putting onto my vagina!"

He said that when I told him that cranberry juice soothes the stinging feeling he presumed that when women have cystitis they ease the harsh pain it can cause by dabbing cranberry juice onto their vaginas!

Something equally stupid he did was when he was going out one day with our youngest daughter when she was first born.

Abby was four months old at the time and my husband had got her ready and put her in her carrier. It was one of those combined carrier and car seat type chairs that had a handle across it for lifting in and out of the car and we also used it in the house for her to snooze in sometimes. So after my husband had strapped her in it he picked her up and said 'bye' to me and walked out of the house and got in the car. I heard him start the engine and as he did I just happened to glance out of the window and I saw that the carrier, with Abby in it, was still on the car roof. So I ran to the front door and just as I opened it he started to drive off up the road! I ran after him shouting and screaming and luckily one of the neighbours heard me and saw Abby on top of the car and flagged my husband down. And when I got alongside him he opened the window and calmly said, "Have I forgotten something"? I said, "Have you FORGOTTEN something???" You COULD say that, yes. Why don't you get out of the car and take a look." And so he did. And when he saw Abby sat on the car roof, happily smiling away, he said, "Oh, I thought she was a bit quiet in the back!"

Being married to my husband sometimes feels like I'm in that television series from years ago called 'Some Mothers Do Ave Em'. And similar to Frank Spencer, the character in it played by Michael Crawford, my husband is also a loving, thoughtful, caring person who always puts his family first and does the best he can for them. Unfortunately, like Frank, he can also be a complete cretin at times.

Horse name

In The Picture For Murder

Owner

Bethany

Story behind the name

I'm originally from Halesowen in the West Midlands and I moved to France when I was twenty four. I used to work in Disneyland Paris where I worked for six years and it's where I met my husband Alain.

We got married at a Chateau in the Dordogne and it was the ideal setting for our wedding. It really was a lovely place, it was idyllic. At the back of it was a river and on the other side of the river were fields that were full of dozens of different coloured flowers and it provided the perfect back drop for our wedding photographs. The only slight drawback with it was that running alongside the river on the other side was a footpath and with it being a lovely sunny day in the middle of August it was quite busy and lots of people were walking up and down the path, so during the photographs we had to wait until people had past so we didn't get them in the shot. This happened several times, and once or twice just as the photographer was about to take a picture someone on the other side would walk into view and we'd have wait until they'd passed and take it again.

We had the usual group photos with all the guests and then me and Alain had ours. The photographer took several pictures like they do and he said he'd send them to us so we could choose the one's we wanted.

The following week he sent the photographs for us to look at and me and Alain picked the ones we wanted, and there was one picture in particular that was a really nice one.

The photographer had caught both Alain and myself at just the right moment. We both looked so happy. And with the river flowing behind us and with the sun glistening off it and with the flowers in the fields behind, it was the perfect picture. The only thing that spoilt it was that just to the edge of it a man had walked into view and he was looking over at us and you could see his face as clearly as you could see mine and Alain's! But seeing as he was right at the edge of the photograph and the photo was 8 x 10 inches, I thought well I can trim it down and it would still be a lovely photograph, so I ordered a print of that one too.

I sent the order back to the photographer and he sent us all the photographs in a wedding album. We had a look through it and when we came to the one with the man in it we both laughed and Alain said it's a pity he's ruined it as it was the best one. So I told him that I was going to trim it down, but I never did, I completely forgot about it and put the wedding album away.

A few weeks later as Alain was reading the local newspaper one day he looked up from it and asked me if I'd trimmed down the photograph with the man in it. I told him that I hadn't and that I'd forgotten all about it and so he asked me to go and get the wedding album. So I went and got it for him. I gave it to him and asked him why he wanted it and he showed me a story he was reading about a man who was murdered a few weeks previously. It was an elderly gentleman who caught an intruder in his house and the intruder beat him to death and then robbed him. The murder took place on the same day we got married less than two miles away from the Chateau and in the newspaper report the police had said that they thought the man had escaped on foot. They gave a description of the suspect and when we looked at the photograph the man in it matched the description they'd given to a tee. It was him. And he was looking directly at the camera.

Alain rang the police and they came around and he gave them the photograph and from it they identified who it was and they traced him and arrested him. The police told us later that the man denied killing the gentleman and said that he was nowhere near the area on that day but the photograph proved otherwise and in the end he admitted to it.

We eventually got the photograph back off the police but I still haven't trimmed it down. Not because I keep forgetting to, I've deliberately kept it like that. It's slightly macabre having a murderer in your wedding photograph but it is a bit of a talking point when we show our wedding album to people. So it's just as well I didn't trim the photograph down when we got the photo's back from the photographer's otherwise the killer may never have been caught.

Horse name

A Brick For A Prick

Owner

Derek

Story behind the name

I read on Martin Lewis's money saving website that some people were paying too much council tax because they'd been put in the wrong council tax band and that it was worth looking into as not only could they be due a refund for the amount they'd overpaid but they'd also be put in the correct band and pay less going forward. So I wrote to my local council saying that I believed I was in the wrong band and could they look into it for me and correct it if need be, and to my delight I received a letter back from them saying that I was indeed in the wrong band and that they would amend it and send me a revised bill and that they'd also refund any overpayments.

I told my neighbours about what the council had said and they too were delighted. They then told other neighbours and soon all the street knew and people were saying well done to me whenever I walked down the street. Not long after I received a letter of confirmation from the council, as did everyone else who lived on our street, and in it they confirmed that we were in the wrong council tax band. However instead of it saying that the amount of council tax we paid was to be reduced it said that it was going to be increased because the band we were in was the one lower than the one we should have been in. Everyone's council tax bill on our street was then increased by £18 a month and instead of being greeted by shouts of 'well done' when I walked down the street I was greeted with shouts of 'you fucking idiot' whenever any of my neighbours saw me. And someone who lived on our street was far less pleased with me than the rest because I woke up one morning to find a brick had been hurled through my front window with 'DICKHEAD' scrawled on it. And so not only did I have to pay more in council tax I also had to fork out £200 for a new double glazing unit.

Thanks a bunch Martin, you prick.

Horse name

Oggy Oggy Oggy

Owner

Nigel

Story behind the name

I was at a car boot sale and I came across one of those battery operated life like cats that you may have seen. They look real and there are various types you can get and this one was a black and white one that was curled up as if it was sleeping. It also had a button underneath it that you can switch on and off and when it's switched on it makes its body go in and out as though it's breathing, and it was that life like that at first glance everyone who saw it thought that it was a real cat. Even close up it looked real and it wasn't until you touched it that you realised it was made of plastic and covered in a material that looks like cat fur.

So I bought it and when I got home I put it on the front lawn and went inside the house. A short while later my wife was looking out of the front window and she said, "Look at that cat asleep in the garden," so I said, "Where?" and got up and had a look. And after I'd looked at it through the window I said to her, "I'm sick to death of cats coming in our garden," and I went outside. And as my wife was watching through the window I ran across the lawn and hoofed it as hard as I could and it flew right across the garden and over the fence into next doors.

My wife looked sickened that I'd just kicked a cat and she banged on the window and shouted, "You rotten bastard!" So I started laughing and walked across the garden and lent over the fence and picked it up took it in and showed her that it wasn't real. She was quite relieved that it wasn't a real cat and as I showed it to her she said, "You better go and tell her it's not real either," and nodded towards the window at one of the neighbours who was stood across the road shaking her head in disgust at how she thought I'd just booted a real cat.

I was going to go out and tell that it wasn't real but when I saw who it was I didn't bother, and that's mainly because she was a right busy body who was always sticking her nose into other people's business. She was the street gossip, a proper 'Hilda Ogden' type who had to know everything what was going on in the street and you'd often see her stood at her garden gate looking up and down the road having a nosey. And when you stopped to speak to her she'd say things like, "Have you heard about them at No.12," or "The police were at No.27 last night. I wonder what was going on." She wanted to know the ins and outs of a cats arse and a week later she saw the insides of one!

In the meantime, two days after I'd hoofed the 'cat' the RSPCA turned up at my house and said they'd received a complaint about animal cruelty. I was baffled when the bloke knocked on and said it as I'd forgot about kicking it but when he said it'd been reported that I'd kicked a cat it dawned on me what he was referring to so I said to him, "Oh, right, come in and I'll explain," but I didn't let on about the cat being a toy one.

We've got a wall mounted electric fire in the front room and the cat was under it and as we walked in I pointed to it and said, "That's the cat there mate. I never wanted it in the first place but my wife insisted we got it," and said, "I can't stand the thing." And I walked over to it and kicked it and it sailed through the air and it hit the patio window and bounced off it and landed on the floor.

He shouted, "Oi, that's enough of that!" So I said, "I'm only messing about, go and look at it," and he did, and just like my wife was, he too was relieved when he saw that it wasn't real.

He wouldn't tell me who'd made the complaint but it was obvious who it was and my wife said that even though she was a right old bag you couldn't blame her for doing it as she'd have thought it was a real cat, which was fair enough I suppose. But as it panned out I got my own back on her anyway for 'reporting' me.

The following Saturday it was a lovely sunny day and a lot of the neighbours and the kids were out in the street, so for a laugh I got the cat and switched it on and went outside and put it under the wheel of my car and got in it and started the engine. I wound all the windows down and put a CD on and turned it up full belt and straight away everyone turned around and looked, including Hilda Ogden, or 'Oggy' as she was known as, who was stood talking shite to one of the neighbours. Funnily enough the CD I put on was a Thin Lizzy one and the song that was playing was 'Don't Believe A Word', which was what you were best off doing whenever gossipmonger Hilda told you anything.

I started revving the engine and as I did Hilda noticed the cat under the wheel and started waving her arms and shouting and pointing at it. Then *all* the neighbours started shouting and pointing at it but I just pretended I hadn't seen them and put my seat belt on as though I was about to pull away. Hilda then started running towards me shouting, "There's a cat under the wheel, don't drive off!" and I leant out of the window and above the music I shouted back, "What? I can't hear you," and at the same time I lifted my foot off the clutch a little bit so the car nudged forward, and she franticly screamed, "STOP!! STOP!! The cat! The cat! It's under your wheel," and pointed at it. And when she got to my car, out of breath from running up the street, she panted, "Oh thank god for that. We all thought you were going to drive off and kill the cat," and she looked down at it breathing in and out under the wheel. And as she was looking at it I said to her, "It's not that black and white one is it by any chance? To which she replied, "Yes, it is." So I said, "Oh good. I can't stand that bleeding thing, it keeps shitting in my garden," and I lifted my foot fully off the clutch and drove over it and crushed it!

Hilda shrieked and turned away not bearing to look as poor old kitty went to meet his maker in pet heaven above. And as I drove away - laughing and meowing out of the window and leaving Hilda stood there being peppered with springs, coils, pieces of plastic, imitation fur and triple AAA batteries - it dawned on her that kitty's maker wasn't in heaven after all and that kitty had actually been Made In China!

Horse name

Freshly Squeezed And Awestruck

Owner

Shay

Story behind the name

I lived in Los Angeles during the early 1980's for several years where I worked for a security company. I was the manager of the company and we provided security for both residential and business clients and one of the places we provided security at was a residential complex called Fremont Place.

Fremont Place is one of Los Angeles' most prestigious enclaves. It was also the first gated community to be built there and some of the most wealthiest people in America lived on the development including King C Gillette the safety razor inventor and A.P. Giannini the founder of The Bank of America. One or two famous people lived there too. It was, and still is, one of the most exclusive places to live in L.A.

Our armed guards patrolled the estate and all the houses had direct links to the main gate where we were located and whenever a call came through or an alarm was triggered we responded. It was rare for an alarm to be activated as only residents and their guests were allowed past the gate. Even the police weren't allowed access without our permission, though it may well be different nowadays. But if an alarm was activated we'd respond immediately and one day an alarm went off so I jumped in my car and headed over to the house where it had been triggered.

When I got out of my car I saw a woman who looked like she was tending the flowers towards the rear of the garden at the side of the house. She was the owner and as soon as she saw me she said that it was a false alarm and that the alarm had been triggered accidentally by her husband.

It was a lovely big house and at the side of it were some stairs that led to the first floor and as she was speaking I heard her husband's voice from behind me saying that there was no need to panic and that everything was cool. And when I turned around I saw Muhammad Ali stood at the top of the stairs.

You could have quite literally knocked me over with a feather. And for a split second I felt awestruck. I'd seen celebrities up close before and I'd met and spoken with a few but to see someone like Muhammad Ali who at the time was possibly the most famous person in the world standing less than fifteen feet away from me was unreal.

He said that he'd set the alarm off unintentionally and that everything was fine and that there was no need for concern. But I explained to him that because the alarm had been activated I had to investigate it thoroughly and that I had to look around his house because he could just be saying that everything is fine because he's been told to say that by an intruder who's holding one of his family hostage at gun point. He said that he understood and he invited me into his house to take a look around.

After I'd had a look around and I was satisfied that everything was okay we started chatting and because he recognised that my accent wasn't an American one (I was born in Dublin and lived in England prior to moving to America) he asked me how I came to be working as a security guard in L.A. I explained to him how it came about and how I used to be a police officer in the UK and whilst holidaying in Los Angeles' eighteen months previous I'd met someone who said that if I ever decided to come and live in L.A. they'd fix me up with a job and so I decided to take him up on his offer. And as we spoke he made me a glass of fresh orange juice which he made from freshly squeezed oranges!

I also visited his house on another occasion and when I went in there were quite a few children in there, but not his. He used to do a lot of work for charity, in particular for underprivileged kids, and these kids were running around his house having the time of their lives jumping on his furniture and climbing on these huge plant like trees he had inside his living room and in other parts of his house. They were having great fun! And another time a woman had made her way passed the gates and she was demanding to see him saying that he was 'the saviour' and she wouldn't leave. She was obsessed with him and kept repeating that he was the saviour and that she had to see him. I think there must have been something wrong with her mentally as she didn't seem quite right. Muhammad must have been informed she was there and he rang the gate and when I answered he said, "Seamus, don't let that mad woman near my house. Get rid of her!!" Someone must have also called the police, possibly one of the other residents, and when they arrived they asked us to remove her as they weren't allowed in as it was private property. I didn't want to cause the woman any distress as she clearly had something wrong with her so I told her that she either left voluntarily and that would be the end of the matter or she'd be arrested and thrown in jail. But she said that she wouldn't leave until she'd seen 'the saviour' and there was no way Mr Ali was coming out of his house! So she was carted off to jail.

But that's the effect Muhammad Ali had on people. He was an icon and to some he truly was their saviour. From mad women to underprivileged kids and everyone in-between, including Presidents, he left lasting impressions on them all. Myself included. And not only could he float like a butterfly and sting like a bee he could also make a mean glass of fresh orange juice! And there probably aren't that many who can say they've had freshly squeezed orange juice made for them by 'The Greatest' as he was known as.

(I also became friends with Hollywood legend Jack Lemmon whilst I was in L.A. but that's another story. And like Muhammad, he too was one of the nicest people you could wish to meet.)

Horse name

The Unsuspecting Mules

Owner

An acquaintance of Billy's

Story behind the name

If you ever went on a family holiday by car to Europe in the late 1970's to the mid 1980's and whilst you were there you had your car stolen and it was quickly found and then when you got back home to England it was stolen again. Or when you were on holiday you thought someone had been in your car and when you got back you thought the same thing had happened again but you never quite knew why, then I'll tell you; you more than likely smuggled drugs back into the country for me.

I was one of the first people, if not *the* first person, in the UK to come up with the idea of using unsuspecting British tourists as 'mules' to bring drugs into the UK. It was dead easy and at the time no-one had done it before and the last people customs thought of checking at Dover and other ports were families, which was the reason we targeted their cars.

There were, and still are, thousands of families who went on holiday by car every year to places like France and Spain and we'd have 'spotters' who when they saw a likely target they'd follow them and when the opportunity arose, such as a petrol station or a roadside cafe or a caravan park (that was the best place) they'd strike up a conversation with them. They'd say that they were on holiday too and ask were the family having a good time, how long were they there for, where were they staying and so on. The mum and dad thought nothing of it as those were the types of questions people ask each other when they meet other people on holiday. But what they didn't realise was they were giving us useful information and then two or three days before their holiday finished their car would go missing one night.

We'd pinch it. And hide drugs inside it.

Usually we'd take the back seat out and hide the drugs in the bottom of the base and then fix the seat back again, or we'd take the side panels off inside the boot. This was a good place to hide it as the boot would be crammed with luggage on the way back and make it even less likely for the drugs to be discovered. We'd then leave their car in a place where it'd easily be found.

The following morning the owners would wake up and see that their car had been stolen and report it missing to the police. The police would find it within a matter of hours, and not think for one minute that drugs had been hidden inside it because it was unheard of back then, and the owners would get it back. And a couple of days later when their holiday was over they'd set off to get the ferry back to England. They'd board the ferry at Calais or wherever they were travelling from and once they arrived in England they'd waltz through customs and drive home. And having got their address from their car registration number, that same night we'd go and pinch their car again and get the drugs.

It was a doddle and we did this for years. Sometimes we didn't even have to steal the car because unlike cars nowadays back in the 70's and 80's you could open most cars by using a metal coat hanger. All you had to do was ease it down the side of the driver's window, hook it around the mechanism and pull it, and you were in. We'd then hide the drugs in it. We used to smuggle it in hire cars as well.

Some families cars weren't big enough to go on holiday in so they'd hire a bigger one instead and we'd get into it, hide the drugs, find out where'd they'd hired the car from by the reg' and the day after they'd taken the car back to the hire company we'd go and hire it again and get the drugs.

In the end the police and customs latched on to it and if ever a car was reported stolen abroad the police in that country would give it a thorough going over, searching it, and using sniffer dogs, until they were satisfied no drugs were hidden inside it before handing it back to the owners. And if drugs were found they'd confiscate them. However, with the co-operation of the British Police and customs and excise, if they did find drugs and it was a large quantity they'd sometimes hand the car back to the owners and not tell them the drugs were in it (which was a bit sneaky) and let them bring it home. They'd then set a trap outside the owner's house and wait for those who had hidden the drugs to come and steal the car again and nick 'em. Fortunately they never caught *us* this way. They never caught me at all actually.

But nothing lasts forever and towards the middle of the 1980's everyone was at it and it was getting far too risky so we stopped doing it but I came up with another way of getting drugs into the country that was just as easy. In fact it was easier as we didn't even need to pinch a car to get the drugs in, we just carried them in.

Ecstasy was huge in the mid to late 80's and early 90's and unlike cannabis which was bulky, ecstasy wasn't, they were tiny pills. And you could make ten times the amount off a handful of ecstasy tablets than you could off a block of weed.

I'd been to watch England play abroad a few times and with the reputation England fans had, causing trouble wherever they went, whatever country we were in they just wanted to get rid of us. And they'd herd fans onto coaches, planes and ferries and get them through customs as quick as they could so as not to cause problems for other passengers. And when I was coming back from one game, as we passed through customs a pal of mine was smoking a joint. The customs people saw him smoking it but none of them said anything to him, they just wanted to get us through, and away. And I thought 'this is an opportunity to smuggle drugs in.'

And back home at airports or ferry ports it was the same. We just gave a quick flash of our passports, which they didn't even bother looking at, and we were through. So I started bringing ecstasy back whenever I went to a football match abroad and not once did I get stopped. I stopped going to the match itself in the end and just travelled with the other fans and used it as a guise to smuggle drugs in.

A few of us were involved in it and looking back the first few times we did it we were taking a bit of a chance as we just used to strap packets of ecstasy containing a thousand tabs in each to our stomachs or on our lower backs and we'd wear chunky type bubble coats to make it look less obvious. We'd split up so it didn't look like we were on a Michelin Man's day out, and even though customs never stopped us at either end I realised it was still too much of a risk as one day they just might, so I came up with other ways of hiding it. One way was to hide it inside the poles of the Union Jack flags that we had that we used to wave at the matches. Or I'd unpick the flag at the edges and hide it in there and glue the edges back up again. It was a lot easier to glue it than stitch it and you couldn't tell it'd been done. Not only that,

I'd have got some very funny looks if I'd have got stopped at Dover on the way out with a needle and cotton! Somehow I don't think customs would've believed me if I'd have told them that I was planning on doing some sewing to pass the time on the ferry journey.

We also used to unpick the stitching on football scarves, which were about 3ft long, and hide the ecstasy in there, and when they were tied in a knot around your neck no-one would have clue that the drugs were hidden inside. Inside the collars on the football shirts we wore was another good place to hide it.

Sometimes I'd pay for a few lads to come with us and as we were going through customs at the ferry ports on the way back I'd get them to kick it off and start trouble as a distraction. I'd make sure that me and the others who had the drugs on us were far away from them near the front and customs would wave us and the other fans straight through. It wasn't only at England matches we did it, we did it at club football matches too and it didn't matter who the team was either. We used to travel with Liverpool fans, Man United fans, Chelsea, Spurs, West Ham fans, all of them, and I probably made more money on each trip than any of their superstar players did in a month.

I'm getting on a bit now, I'm touching seventy, and I'm not exactly proud of being involved in drugs when I was younger. Though I suppose I do have a sense of being innovational having come up with the idea's I did to smuggle the drugs in. And if I caused anyone any inconvenience or stress by pinching their car when they were holidaying on the continent all those years ago then I apologise to them and their family.

Horse name

I'd Kill For A Good Night's Sleep

Owner

Lillian

Story behind the name

There's always been a history of sleepwalking in our family. *I* used to do it. My brother used to do it. My father used to do it, and now my daughter does it as well. The difference is that when my brother, my father and I used to do it we never tried to murder anyone whereas my daughter has tried to kill *me* on several occasions.

Sleepwalking affects people in different ways. Some people get up and make a drink or get something to eat. Others will just walk around the house and then get back in bed again and some will sit up and talk and have a full blown conversation with themselves. But me and my brother and my father did more than just walk and talk in our sleep.

My mother told me that she once woke up shivering in the middle of the night and when she got out of bed and turned the light on she saw that all the bed sheets and the duvet and my dad's pillow cases had been removed and she couldn't see them anywhere. She couldn't see my father either. So she went downstairs where she found him bending down in front of the washing machine putting all the bedding in it. He'd decided to wash the bedding in his sleep! And another time when my mother woke up and realised that my father had slept walked she went downstairs to find him doing the ironing. The only thing was that he wasn't actually ironing any clothes. He'd just got the ironing board out and the iron and he was going up and down the board with it. My mother said that my father never did the washing or the ironing when he was awake so why he decided to do it in his sleep is anyone's guess!

My mother was also woken one night by the sound of Alger, our pet dog, barking. And when she went downstairs she found my brother on his hands and knees eating Alger's food out of his bowl! And when I was five years old my mother heard my bedroom door opening one night so she got up as she knew that I might have been sleepwalking and she saw me going down the stairs. She followed me down and I went into the kitchen and took Alger out of his dog bed and took him back upstairs and put him in *my* bed. I then went back down again and got in his bed and curled up into a ball like dogs do and carried on sleeping. This happened on more than one occasion. Poor old Alger must have got really fed up being turfed out of his bed and having his food eaten in the middle of the night!

My dad and my brother and I used to do funny things like that in our sleep all the time but when my own daughter started sleepwalking, in the end, the things she did weren't so funny.

She started doing it when she was eight years old and she'd routinely do the same thing, and that was walk in our bedroom and stand by the side of the bed. I've lost count of the amount of times she's done it and she always stood by my side, never by my husband's side of the bed, and she just used to stand there staring at me with a kind of contorted angry look on her face. This was how it started off and the first time it happened it really startled me. I must have sensed that something was next to me and when I opened my eyes she was stood right by the edge of the bed looking down at me with a weird look on her face as though she was annoyed with me.

I got used to it in the end but one night I awoke feeling as though something was pressing down on my face and I couldn't breathe properly and my face felt really warm and I couldn't see anything. And the reason was, was because my daughter was holding a pillow over my face and was leaning on it.

It was as though she was trying to smother me. I shouted and pushed her off me and she woke up and burst into tears. My husband woke up too and we put her back to bed and the following morning she had no recollection of it. Me and my husband laughed it off and he said that he'd often thought about smothering me himself when I was asleep. But when it kept happening and the things she did became more frightening it was no laughing matter.

One night I was awoken by an almighty whack on my head. And then I felt another whack, and then another. And when I jumped out of bed and put the bedroom light on I saw my daughter stood there with our bedside lamp in her hand and even though I was no longer in the bed she was whacking the pillow with it. She did a similar thing with the lamp a few nights later too and I woke to find her holding the flex on it across my throat. But the most frightening one was when my husband woke up one night to find her stood over me holding a pair of scissors. I was fast asleep and knew nothing about it but luckily my husband had woken needing to use the bathroom and he saw her stood there holding the scissors in both hands above her head over me. He said it reminded him of the type of scene you see in a horror movie about Satan or Devil worshipers where there's a girl lying on the alter about to be sacrificed and someone's stood over her holding a dagger above her chest.

My daughter had picked the scissors up off the chest of drawers in our bedroom, how long she'd been stood there with them above her head we don't know. Thankfully she didn't bring them down on me and my husband quickly got out of bed and took them off her and put her back in her own bedroom.

That was when we decided to seek help and we contacted doctors, sleep disorder specialists and even a psychiatrist, none of whom could explain why my daughter would want to try and kill me. It's not as if I was very strict with her or if I'd punished her for something she'd done and it'd stuck in her head in her subconscious. I was far from strict with her and I hardly ever told her off as she was a very well behaved child. The doctors, like us, were baffled why she was doing it.

In the end we found a simple solution, we put a hook lock at the top of my daughter's bedroom door on the outside to stop her getting out. And whenever she did try to get out we could hear her door rattling as she tried to open it, and for extra piece of mind we put one on the inside of our bedroom door too. I was then able to sleep peacefully without worrying that I'd be garrotted, smothered or sacrificed during the night.

Horse name

Awfully Funny

Owner

Ian

Story behind the name

Dementia is awful. And if you know of someone who has suffered from it or who *is* suffering from it then you'll know just how awful it is. But as distressing and as upsetting as it can be, not only for the person who has got it but for other family members too, every now and then there can be some humorous moments, which can either be something the person who is suffering from it says or something they do. My mum suffers from dementia. She's eighty six and she's had it for several years now and there have been several such humorous moments. One of which was quite touching too.

She still lives at home by herself and one morning my sister went around to see her at about 9 am. It was the day of Prince Harry's wedding and my mum has always enjoyed watching royal ceremonies such as the trooping of the colour and the Queen's birthday parade. So my sister told her that she could go to hers in the afternoon and watch it. The reason she said that she could go to hers and watch it was apart from it being a bit of company for mum my sister had a big fifty inch widescreen television whereas my mum has only got a small twenty four inch one that she's had for years and so the picture would be much better on my sister's.

When my sister told my mum, my mum said, "Oh that'll be lovely, thanks. I'll look forward to that," and so my sister told her that she'd come and get her at about 12 o'clock.

My sister lives literally over the road from my mum and so at ten to twelve she walked over to get her. She knocked on the front door and when my mum opened it my sister was slightly taken aback by what my mum had on.

She'd got changed from what she was wearing earlier in the morning and she was now dressed in her best dress. She also had her best shoes on. And she was wearing a matching hat that matched the dress and shoes and she was wearing a pair of dress gloves. (We've no idea where she dug those up from.) She also had a matching handbag that hadn't been seen for years. The only thing that was missing was a red carnation! And with a beaming smile on her face my mum said, "I'm all ready!" She'd misunderstood what my sister had said to her in the morning and she thought that she was going to the actual wedding itself! My sister thought well with the size of her tele' it'll be like being there anyway and my mum won't know much difference. So she just said, "C'mon then, we don't want to be late do we."

When they got to my sister's house it was as my sister thought, my mum didn't notice any difference and just sat down in front of the television and started watching it, though more than likely she'd just forgotten that she thought she was going to it even though it was less than ten minutes since she thought she was. Although when my sister's husband walked in the living room, barefoot in his joggers and T shirt, my mum said to him, "You could have at least made an effort!"

Unfortunately, moments like that with my mum are few and far between and they are now becoming even less frequent and more often than not the things she says and does are distressing as opposed to funny. What makes it worse for my mum is that she has a form of dementia where she knows that what she's saying or doing isn't right, so it's even more frustrating for her. And sometimes she'll be in tears crying and banging her head with her hand saying 'what's wrong with me' because she's aware that some of the things she does or her forgetfulness isn't normal. Whereas other people who suffer from it don't know any difference and think that the things they say and do are perfectly normal, which in one way is a blessing as it's not as frustrating for them. Either way, dementia truly is a cruel, terrible disease and the frightening thing is that more and more people are getting it. Even more frightening is that there isn't a cure in sight. So if you do know someone who suffers from it, when lighter moments like the one I've just told you about come along make the most of them because for every lighter moment they'll be a thousand awful ones.

*My mum died shortly after I wrote this story, and so if any of you have got a loved one who suffers with dementia I sympathise with you. Dementia truly is an awful disease. I've seen (and done) things that no son should have to see or do for their mum, and I won't be the only one. They'll be thousands of other sons, and daughters too, who have to do things for their mum's and dad's that they really shouldn't have too. But we do those things because we don't forget the things our mum's and dad's did for us.

Horse name

My Dad's A Dick

Owner

Billy

Story behind the name

My dad committed suicide when I was in my mid twenties. He killed himself not long after splitting up with my mum and it was a mixture of depression, living alone in a crappy bedsit - which must have been hard for him after all those years of living as part of a family in a nice house - alcohol and the epilepsy that he suffered from which prompted him into doing it. Although he never let his epilepsy get in the way of his ambition of becoming a paratrooper when he was in his late teens and he didn't tell them about it when he applied and the tit jumped out of a plane at 10,000ft knowing he could've blacked out before having chance to open his parachute and plummeted to his death! He had some bottle to say the least to do something like that, even though it was a fairly stupid thing to do. And it wasn't until he had one of his 'blackouts' in front of one of the officers that it ended his hopes of wearing the Red Beret.

But like a lot of father and son relationships can sometimes be, me and my dad didn't always see eye to eye. Our relationship was alright when I was a young kid up to the age of around thirteen or fourteen and I've got a lot of fond memories from those years, but after that things started to deteriorate. His alcohol problem and him being unemployed - which meant he was at home most days (when he wasn't in the pub) - didn't help matters either.

My dad was one of those "Do as I say not as I do types" and everything was on his terms and everything was done in his own time and when it suited him, everything revolved around *him* kind of thing. Basically, he was a fucking selfish pig-headed cunt! And this is an example *of* his pig-headedness. It's quite amusing too.

When I was younger we used to go to a place called Rhyl in North Wales for our holidays. Rhyl was alright when I was I kid. It's gone downhill now but at the time it was great. Everyone went there. Most of the people I know who are my age used to go there for their holidays.

We used to go every year. We used to go on the train as my dad didn't drive because of his epilepsy. And as I've mentioned he liked a drink too. So it's just as well he *didn't* drive because epilepsy, alcohol and cars aren't a particularly good mix! So rather than get in a car with an epileptic piss head behind the wheel we stuck to the train instead. And one year as we boarded the train my dad decides to get off to get a newspaper and I remember my mum saying to him, "No, Barry, don't. It's leaving in a minute," and he turned around and in his slow, deliberate tone that he spoke with he said to my mum, "It'll *wait* for me." And although I was only six years old at the time even *I* knew it wouldn't wait for him and I looked at him thinking "I bet it fucking doesn't you silly cunt!"

But the daft bastard got off anyway and went to get a paper and as he was casually strolling back to the train with his Daily Express under his arm the train began to pull away. And he stopped and looked at it like he was in disbelief that the driver had the audacity to leave without him. And as I looked out of the window I could see him berating someone from British Rail on the platform because the train had gone without him. He was unbelievable. He actually thought the train would wait for him, like the driver would be sat there thinking, "Fuck the timetable and fuck everybody else on the train, we can't leave because Barry has to get his Daily Express."

My dad finally turned up in Rhyl three hours later after catching the next train although he may as well have stayed where he was because after we'd unpacked and were strolling down the seafront we saw a coach with 'Mystery Tour' on it. So we asked my dad if we could get on it and he said yes and two and a half hours later we were at Belle Vue in Gorton in Manchester which was about two miles away from where we lived! My dad had nodded off on the coach and woke up just as we arrived and when he saw where we were I heard him mutter, "I don't fucking believe it."

Belle Vue by the way for those who aren't old enough to remember it or haven't heard of it was just like Blackpool pleasure beach. It had roller coasters, rides, water slides, fun fairs and a zoo. It also had a concert hall where a lot of the big names and bands played, Rod Stewart being one of them.

My dad's "do as I say not as I do" attitude was quite irritating at times. It's more of an older generation's attitude towards their kids although a lot of modern day parents still have it. Personally I think it's the wrong attitude for parents to have. If one of your kids sees you do something and they copy you and do the same thing and you tell them off for doing it they're going to think, "Well you fucking do it so why can't I!"

My dad was born in Liverpool and he was a fanatical Liverpool supporter and I remember going to Anfield with him one day to watch them play. And when we were on the train (fortunately he'd bought a newspaper before we boarded it otherwise I'd have probably ended up in Liverpool on my own!) there were a group of kids aged around fourteen or fifteen sat on the opposite side of us who were smoking. I was about eleven at the time and my dad said to me, "Don't ever let me catch *you* smoking. It's not good for you." He then reached in his jacket pocket, took out his fags and lit one up! He used to smoke twenty Senior Service - one of the strongest fags there were - a day and there he was lecturing *me* on the dangers of smoking! Perhaps the warning that's on cigarette packets that says "Cigarettes can seriously damage your health" should also have underneath it, "And parents life advice can seriously fucking confuse kids!"

As well as my dad's "Do as I say" attitude being quite irritating, something else that irritated me was his insistence that there had to be a cup of coffee ready and waiting for him by his armchair when he came in from the pub at night. And what was irritating even more was that he didn't *say* for us to do it. He just gave a 'signal' - via telephone.

When he'd left the pub, which was usually around eleven o'clock at night after he'd had a skinful, he'd walk over to the phone box opposite the pub and ring home. But he wouldn't be ringing to speak to anyone. He'd be ringing to give a signal that he was on his way home and for someone to put the kettle on and make him a cup of coffee, which like I say, had to be ready and waiting for him placed by his armchair when he got in.

I kid you not!

What my dad used to do was ring the house phone, let it ring twice, and then put the phone down. And we'd be sat at home watching the television and we'd hear the house phone go 'Brr Brr - Brr Brr,' and that was our signal for one of us to get up and put the kettle on and make him a cup of Mellow Birds.

'Brr Brr' isn't a very good description of a phone ringing I know but I couldn't think of any other way of describing the sound it made!

My dad didn't always drink Mellow Birds coffee. He'd sometimes have that Camp coffee. Do you remember it? It's still around now I think. It's a liquid coffee that comes in a bottle. It's like a dark brown syrup and it comes out like runny wet shit when you pour it in the cup. It tastes like runny wet shit as well!

Anyhow, the phone box opposite the pub where my dad would ring from was about a five minute walk from our house and so by the time he got in his coffee would be ready. But then what he started doing was giving 'two buzzes' as he called it from a phone box that was *even nearer* our house. It was literally around the corner from where we lived. And I do mean *literally* around the corner. It was *two* corners to be precise. And to be *very precise* it was exactly 172 yards from the front door. (I've actually strode it out!)

And if you want a better idea for yourself of just how close the phone box was that my dad used to ring from, the next time you leave your house to go to the shops or to go for a walk count 172 strides from when you step out of your front door and you'll see just how close to home my dad used to be when he rang. The phone box was that close that the kettle hadn't even boiled by the time he'd got home! In fact it was that close we barely had time to unscrew the lid off the Mellow Birds and put a spoonful in the cup - or pour some runny wet liquid shit coffee substitute in the cup depending on which we made - let alone boil the kettle and add the milk and sugar and make it!

My dad was in his fifties when he killed himself though I think our neighbours must have thought he'd done it long before that on one occasion. Either that or they must have thought that someone in the family had died - and all because his beloved Liverpool had lost the 1971 F.A. Cup final to Arsenal. And to make matters worse the player he hated most, Arsenal striker Charlie George, scored the winning goal. And he hated him mainly because he had long hair!

My dad was 'old school'. He was always tidy in his appearance; clean shaven, trimmed hair - slicked back with Brylcreem (that white greasy shit that was in a red tub) - shirt tucked in, tie, trousers, polished shoes, etc. Not forgetting a dab of Old Spice! 'Sunday Best' kinda thing, like the older generation of blokes used to dress in those days. And Charlie George was the opposite, he was a bit *un*shaven and "slovenly looking" as my dad described him, and he played with his shirt hanging out, which my dad didn't like. My dad was of the opinion that a shirt, even those worn by footballers, should be tucked in. Charlie George also had long hair which my dad couldn't stand on a bloke. And when Charlie boy knocked in the winner with seconds to go my dad went berserk. He shouted, "The scruffy long haired bastard!" and he jumped out of his armchair (knocking his coffee over as he did so which made him even more annoyed!) and ran over to the television and put his foot straight through it. And it exploded! And at the final whistle - not that we saw the referee *blow* his whistle because the screen was shattered, though we did *hear* him blow it from the speaker that was hanging out of the set - my dad drew the front room curtains and we all had to sit in total darkness for the rest of the weekend! (That's what people used to do in those days, draw the curtains when someone in the family had passed away. Hence the neighbours thinking someone had died.) It was like he was in mourning! I was half expecting a wreath to be lying on the step when I opened the front door the following day when I went out to do my paper round!

My dad also did a daft thing that may well have left another Liverpool supporter feeling suicidal.

It was a Saturday and he'd been to watch Liverpool play at Anfield. I was sat in the living room and at about nine o'clock at night I heard him walk in through the front door. Well he didn't exactly *walk* through the front door. He stumbled and staggered through it. He then tripped over the mat and fell flat on his face. Pissed! I then heard my mum shout, "What the bloody hell is that?"

I thought, "Fucking hell. He must be in a right state if his own wife can't even recognise him!"

I then heard a "Woof" and when I stuck my head around the door I saw my dad lying face down in the hallway with a Golden Retriever sat next to him! And as he's lying there, paralytic, with a Labrador that I'd never seen before sat by his side, I looked at him thinking, "Well I know they give Labradors to the blind but I never knew they gave them to the *blind drunk* as well!" But no one *had* given it to him. He'd just seen it and thought, "I'll have that," and took it and brought it home with him. From Liverpool! And as my dad got to his knees he stroked its head, ruffled its fur and slurred, "I love Labradors. They're my favourite type of dog."

Well BMW's are my favourite type of car but I wouldn't go out and fucking nick one!

The following day, when he'd sobered up, he told us that he'd seen it sat on its own outside Lime Street station in Liverpool and thought, "What a lovely dog that is," and picked it up and got on the train with it and brought it home, like you would! Or like a fucking dickhead would! Some poor Scouser had probably only let it off its lead for a piss and it's wondered off, got lost and ended up forty miles away in Manchester. Which rubs it in even more for the poor Scouser – having his dog nicked by a Manc'! And guess what my dick of a dad called it? Fucking Scouse!!

I don't mean he called it *fucking* Scouse. That *would've* been stupid, even for my dad. He just named it 'Scouse' - which was fucking stupid enough. I used to feel a right prick shouting, "Here Scouse," as it ran off when I was taking it for a walk. Which it did on many occasions. More than likely trying to find its way back to Liverpool! It must have been thinking, "Where the fuck am I? And why does this stupid twat keep on calling me Scouse!" I just hope it wasn't also thinking, "And where's that other bloke gone that I used to live with that wore dark sunglasses and used to tap a white stick on the ground when we were out walking!"

Looking back now - because you don't really understand what a person is going through when you're a young kid - it must have been really frustrating for my dad. He'd had to stop doing his job because of his epilepsy. He was a band-knife cutter in the clothing trade and he'd sliced off his thumb and severed all the tendons in his arm on the saw machine when he'd blacked out after he'd had an epileptic fit. And because of his epilepsy he was limited to what he could do for a job, and unemployment was high around that time too which made it doubly hard for him trying to find work. He couldn't drive because of his epilepsy, which limited him further. And he was on medication for it too. And as I've mentioned he also suffered with depression and he'd tried twice to commit suicide before he eventually did it. In the end he sought solace in the booze and once the alcohol had got a grip of him he was fucked. And it eventually fucked our relationship up and then fucked the family up too - before finally fucking *him* up. So much so he took his own life.

Some may find this a bit warped but I actually joke about my dad killing himself. And before I was sent to prison many years ago my probation officer said that me joking about my dad's suicide was my way of dealing with it. She was wrong. It wasn't. I'm just a sick cunt! And she, and a few others since, agreed I *was* a sick cunt when I told the story that I made up about it! I was even told so by one person on one occasion. And had a drink thrown over me into the bargain!

There were a load of us on holiday in Magaluf and we were chatting to this group of girls, women. One of them was a bereavement counsellor and I was telling her about my dad killing himself. I told her that I was the one that found him. I wasn't, I just *said* that I was. And she said, "Oh dear. That must have been awful for you." So I said, "Yes, it was a bit of a shock," and said, "I remember opening the door to his flat and seeing him hanging from the lampshade with a rope around his neck wearing stockings and suspenders and a peep-hole bra with an orange in his mouth. And there was a three legged stool on the floor underneath him that he'd been balancing on that he'd sawn one of the legs off that had fallen over." My mates started laughing but she didn't twig that I was joking and in a stern voice she said to them, "You shouldn't laugh. It isn't funny." I then said to her, trying like fuck not to laugh, "My dad used to get his kicks out of playing risky sex games. Apparently, if you ejaculate whilst on the verge of choking it's more intense and that's what he'd been doing. But I was unsure if he was dead." And she said, "Oh my god. That must have been horrific to see. What did you do? Cut the rope and get him down and phone for an ambulance?" So I said, "No. I went over to him and put the stool back under his feet, put his cock back in his hand and said to him "Carry on wanking if you want Dad. Don't mind me. I'll go and make a cup of tea. Gimme a shout when you've finished." She then realised I was taking the piss! And she didn't find it funny - unlike all my mates who were laughing like fucking hyenas! And she said, "You fucking sick bastard!" And she stood up, picked up her drink and threw it all over me and stormed off!

My dad committing suicide didn't really affect me emotionally and on a scale of 1 - 100 where most people's grief for a loved one who had committed suicide would be at a hundred mine was only around three. Sad, but true. Though a pal of mine's grief was off the scale when it happened to him.

I've always been of the opinion that you should "be your own man" (or woman) and if someone doesn't like you for who or what you are then bollocks to 'em! I used to tell my kids the same thing when they were growing up, for them to be themselves and not to worry about others. My mate Kenny used to say the same to his son Ethan and he said that he thought Ethan was of the same view too. However Ethan was putting on a front and deep down he didn't think he was good enough for anyone or *anything*. Ethan was a nice kid and Kenny said that not for one second did he suspect that anything was wrong in Ethan's life or that he had any problems. He was doing well at university, he'd set goals for what he wanted to achieve in his life and he was his usual happy go lucky self, seemingly without a care in the world. Then one day, for no apparent reason, he killed himself. He was just nineteen. Obviously there *was* a reason why Ethan took his own life but what that reason was only Ethan knew and agonisingly for his mum and dad they'll never know, though one thing that Kenny thinks played a part was social media. We live in a world that revolves around social media. People are obsessed with it, in particular teenagers. They're glued to their phones for hours on end looking at things on Snapchat, Tik Tok, Instagram and Facebook. And most of what they look at is utter fucking shite. Then you've got YouTubers and Influencers - most of whom are a *bad influence*. And add to that keyboard warriors, trolls, bullies, sick bastards, vindictive arseholes and spineless shitbags, Kenny may well be right saying social media contributed to Ethan taking his own life. Some people reading will probably think, "Old fart! What does he fucking know. He needs to move with the times. Social media is part of life." And it is. And there are good things about it. But there are a lot of bad things about it too. And for me you can shove things like Snapchat, Instagram Tik Tok and Facebook up your fucking arse. And one thing's for certain, if there weren't social media platforms like those there'd be far less 'Ethans' and far less parents whose lives have been shattered. And far less parents would be worrying about what their kids are viewing online. Kids are impressionable, some more than others, and they see things - and people - on social media and think, "I wish I was like that" or "I wish I had that kind of life." And depending on their personality, and state of mind, it can make them think their own life is shit. And over time things build up and eventually they get to the point where they think their life isn't worth living. And that's what Kenny thinks happened to Ethan. It may only happen to one kid in a hundred thousand but it's still one kid too many.

One thing that Kenny said he found hard to comprehend about Ethan killing himself was that the night before he did it they'd been to see Ricky Gervais in concert. He said that Ethan was in hysterics laughing all the way through it, and he said that he'd never seen him happier. But then less than 24 hours later he killed himself. I find that hard to comprehend myself too though apparently when someone has decided that they're going to commit suicide they're content, happy even, in the days before they do it because they've got peace of mind that the problems and issues they've got will soon be over.

At least Ethan died happy I suppose. It could've been worse. Instead of going to see Ricky Gervais, Kenny could have took Ethan to one of those 'woke' comedy nights that they have these days that are popular with the "trendy's" and the politically correct. Ethan wouldn't have laughed *once* if he'd have gone to one of them let alone been in hysterics. He'd have probably topped himself halfway through the fucking show they're that unfunny! Though he probably wouldn't have made it to halfway. Those woke comedy nights are that shit Ethan would've more than likely hung himself five minutes into it!! Though saving said I find it hard to comprehend Ethan doing that, thinking about it, in a way, I *can* comprehend it.

In the story 'Double The Heartache' Julian tells of how his best friend killed himself even though seemingly nothing was wrong. And an old mate of mine did the very same thing. He too was in the pub with all of his mates and at the end of the night when he left he said to one of the lads he worked with that he'd see him in the morning. And when his mate called at his house to pick him up for work the following day and got no answer when he knocked on for him he went around the back of the house and looked through the kitchen window where he saw Olly' hanging from the kitchen ceiling. My dad also seemed his normal self when I saw him the week before *he* killed himself. His was pissed but he was his normal self! Though being pissed *was* his normal self! So it just goes to show that even though someone *appears* to be in good state of mind they may well not be.

But for all of his faults my dad was a pretty good judge of character and this is a good example.

I was around the same age as I was in the 'train story' when he decided to get off and get a newspaper, five or six years old. And at around three o'clock on a Saturday night / Sunday morning when I was asleep in bed I was awoken by the sound of the front door opening. My dad had just finished work. He worked on the doors in town, in Manchester. He was a 'bouncer', a doorman at pubs and clubs. And as he came in I could hear him talking to someone. I heard another man's voice too. I fell back to sleep and ten minutes later I was woken up again by these strange noises coming from downstairs. I'd never heard these noises before in our house. It was a 'tutting' type noise, as though someone was tutting very quickly, like a "tut-tut-tut-tut-tut-tut." And they were followed by little squealing noises. And having never heard them before I was curious as to what they were. So I got out of bed and quietly crept downstairs.

I went into the kitchen and slowly pushed open the door that led into the living room and peeped around it. And when I did I saw my dad sat in the arm chair and some bloke who I'd never seen before sat on the settee opposite him. They were both naked and my dad was putting a condom on and the bloke was taking the lid off a jar of Vaseline.

I'm only joking!

They weren't really. It's just my slightly twisted sense of humour kicking in! It's just as well my dad's dead or else he'd have battered me if he knew I'd written that about him!

So as I'm looking at my dad and this bloke sitting there (fully clothed) I heard the tutting noises again coming from somewhere above my head and when I looked up at the ceiling I saw a monkey swinging off the lampshade! And I pushed the door wide open and ran in the living room and started jumping up and down laughing my head off and shouting, "IT'S A MONKEY! IT'S A MONKEY! at the top of my voice"

It was a little chimp. And it looked down at me, swung off the lampshade, jumped onto the picture rail, flew across on to the top of the living room door and dropped down onto my head and started yanking and pulling at my ears! Which could well be the reason why I ended up with such big lug holes! (There's more on my big ears in my 'Dropping Dad In It' story'.)

I thought it was brilliant but my mum was less than impressed when she came downstairs after hearing the commotion and me shouting at the top of my voice to find some strange bloke she'd never seen before sat in her living room and her six year old son rolling around on the carpet in fits of laughter having his ears torn off by a chimpanzee!

It turned out that this bloke was from out of town and that he was going around the pubs in Manchester telling people he was a professional photographer and asking them if they wanted their photograph taken with his monkey and charging them a fiver for one. The only problem was there was no film in his camera! He wasn't a professional photographer at all. He was a professional con-man! But even though my dad knew he was a con-man, and despite the fact he'd never met him before and knew nothing about him, because the bloke had missed his last train home my dad said he could get his head down at our house for the night. It's no wonder my mum wasn't happy when you think about it. She had three kids in the house, as well as herself, and my dad had brought some strange bloke back who he'd never even met before to stay the night. The bloke could've been anybody. A murderer. A rapist. A paedophile. A violent psychopath. You never know do you?

But as I said, my dad must have been a pretty good judge of character because although the bloke was a con-man he was also half decent and he appreciated what my dad had done for him, and we got up in the morning to find that he'd already gone and that he'd left a tenner on the sideboard as a thank you. It would've been nice if he'd have left a photograph of the monkey for me too as a keepsake. But then again he wouldn't have been able to would he because there was no fucking film in his camera!

Horse name

Swallowed Alive

Owner

Eddie

Story behind the name

I was in the army nearly all my life and I've witnessed things that'll stick in my mind until the day I die. I've served in Iraq and Afghanistan where I saw some fairly gruesome sights including the aftermath of suicide bombers and car bombs being detonated which left dead bodies and body parts strewn across the street. And I've seen good friends get shot and killed right in front of me. And as horrific and gruesome as these images were, and still are whenever they come into my mind, there's one image above all others that even though it wasn't as horrific or gruesome as some of the things I've seen, it sticks in my mind more than anything else. Although as I'm sure you'll agree after you've read it, it must have been EXTREMELY horrific at the time for the person involved.

We were on a training exercise in the jungle in Southeast Asia and although there was no human threat in the form of enemies or terrorists, there *was* a threat from the various species of animals and creatures that inhabited the jungle, one of which was the threat of snakes, some of which were highly venomous. Just one bite from a couple of snakes in particular that were known to inhabit the area of the jungle we were in could've resulted in death within minutes. Needless to say we trod very carefully when we were walking through the jungle.

During the day the heat and humidity in the jungle was unbearable at times, it really was. And it could be equally unbearable at night time when you were lying in your tent in your sleeping bag trying to get to sleep. Some of the guys didn't bother using their sleeping bags because it was just too hot. But others, like me, did. Because even though the chances of a snake slithering into your tent at night were slim due to the way the tents were designed to prevent things crawling in, it was still in the back of your mind that one just might find its way in. So, better safe than sorry, I always slept in my sleeping bag. However one of the guys in our unit who didn't use his sleeping bag was Brian and one night whilst we were sleeping we were woken by his screams and his frantic cries of "Help" coming from inside his tent. So like everyone else I immediately got up and ran over to his tent and when we ripped his tent open I couldn't quite believe my eyes at what I saw.

We could see Brian and the top half of his body. And we could see his left leg. But we couldn't see his right leg. And that's because it was inside the mouth of an 18ft python which had swallowed it right up to his groin. The look on Brian's face was one of sheer terror, as it would be if you woke up to find yourself being swallowed alive by an 18ft python, and he was screaming, "Get it off me. Get it off me."

The tent was about 7ft long and there was at least another 12ft of the python trailing out of the tent. Someone shouted to get a machete. Fortunately there was one to hand in Brian's tent as we'd been using them to cut through the jungle on our treks. So we told Brian to stretch his left leg out so that we roughly knew where his right foot was inside the python, and we added on another couple of foot so we didn't cut his right foot off, and then we chopped the python in half.

As the machete went through it Brian shouted out in pain and at first we thought that we'd somehow chopped through his foot as well. But we then realised that we hadn't chopped into his foot and that the python, in reaction to the shock of it being hit with the machete, had sunk its teeth into Brian's thigh. Though I think Brian was in a much greater state of shock than the snake. We then cut the python open and got Brian's leg out, much to his relief.

How the snake got in was a bit of a mystery as Brian said he was sure that he'd secured his tent as you're supposed to do when camping in the jungle. But somehow the snake got in. And he said that as he was sleeping something stirred him and he was woken slightly by an 'itching' feeling on his thigh and so he scratched it. But he said that as he scratched his leg he couldn't feel the scratching so he scratched it harder, and even though he was scratching his leg quite hard he still couldn't feel it and the itching feeling was still there. And when he looked down at his leg he realised *why* he couldn't feel himself scratching it - he was scratching the top of pythons head!

It's no wonder he had a look of sheer terror on his face when we ripped his tent open. Imagine the fear you'd feel at not only seeing that an 18ft python was swallowing you, you actually had your hand on its head.

He was very lucky on two counts really. A, that it wasn't one of the highly venomous snakes that we were warned about that had slithered into his tent and bit his leg because he most certainly would've died if it had have been. And B, not only was it fortunate that pythons aren't venomous it was also fortunate that it only swallowed *one* of his legs because when it got to his groin it couldn't go any further. If it had swallowed *both* of his legs he may not have been so lucky as it could've quite easily swallowed all of him, alive, something which has happened to quite a few of the locals in places like Southeast Asia and India.

As you might have guessed, Brian slept in his sleeping bag every night for the rest of the expedition. He also checked, and then double checked, that his tent was properly secured and zipped up before he bedded down for the night.

Horse name

Peeved Parents

Owner

Craig

Story behind the name

Like many parents who have been fined for taking their kids out of school during term time to go on holiday I was a little bit 'peeved' when I received an education penalty notice from the council informing us that me and my wife were to be fined £120 for doing so. And not only was I a little bit peeved to have been issued with a penalty notice as I thought my holiday request was a reasonable one, it also riled me that the cheeky bastards at my local council had the gall to suggest we take our SUMMER holidays at either the half term at the beginning of March or the half term at the end of October. (I'd asked to take my son out of school so we could go away at the end of June and told them when I made the request that I couldn't go throughout the summer holidays in August as I was working away, hence them suggesting we take our summer holiday in March or October.)

I appealed the fine and lost so I paid it. I was a bit gutted actually, not just because I had to pay it but because I wanted to pay it in pennies and I was going to take a hundred and twenty pounds worth down to the council offices in a wheelbarrow and tip in reception, but they didn't accept cash at the council offices so had to write a cheque instead. And so when I sent them the cheque I enclosed a letter with it asking if anyone at the council took *their* summer holidays in March or October and pointed out that in Majorca where we go for our holiday that at those times of the year hardly any bars, restaurants, waterparks etc are open. And I said that if any of them had been to Majorca in March they'd also know that the weather is pretty shite then and more often than not it's cold, wet and pissing down. And I finished by saying that the hotel pool is usually icy cold too at that time of year and that I really didn't fancy spending a week freezing my bollocks off every time I jumped in it. And I thanked them for suggesting we take our summer holiday in early March or late October but that we'd stick to going around June/July time if it was all the same to them. They didn't reply.

As those of you who have received penalty notices will know, apart from outlining what are classed as 'exceptional circumstances' for which schools will authorise the holiday request it also says how important it is for kids to attend school at all times and that even having a couple of days off can be detrimental to a child's education. Well if that's the case and they *are* so concerned for our kids education why do teachers go on strike during term time forcing our kids to miss school for a couple of days? And why do some schools close at dinner time several times a year to 'prepare' for opening evenings and parents evenings (all they've got to do is put a few tables out in the main hall.) And why do they have 'inset days' or teacher training days four or five times a year during term time instead of having them during the school holidays, when presumably the teachers are still getting paid. And it's perfectly acceptable for them to send us a text message at eight o'clock in the morning in the middle of February informing us that we can keep our kids off school because it's snowing. And it's also acceptable - and even more infuriating - for them to send us a text message at 11 o'clock *mid* morning when the kids are already *in* school saying that they're shutting the school at dinner time because of the snow! Apparently, the reason they do this is because the teachers will have difficulty getting home because the roads and traffic are bad. But does everybody else's place of work shut at dinner time so *we* can get home? No, they don't. So why should schools be allowed to do it? Let the teachers sit in traffic for two fucking hours like the rest of us have to.

Talk about one rule for the parents and another for the schools. When it suits *them* for our kids to have time off during term time it's absolutely fine but when *we* want to do it it's not. And if they're so concerned about our kids missing school because it's detrimental to their education then they wouldn't do any of what I've just mentioned would they? The schools and local councils are hypocrites. And what makes me laugh - actually it doesn't make me laugh it makes me quite fucking annoyed - is that teachers go on strike during term time for the same reason parents take their kids out of school during term time to go on holiday: money. Teachers strike for more of it and parents take their kids out of school to save it. The only difference is that teachers are allowed to do it. So if it's illegal for *us* to take our kids out of school during term time for financial reasons it should also be made illegal for teachers to go on strike for financial reasons during term time as well. It's only fair, surely?

As I mentioned, I thought our reasons for asking to take our son out of school to go on holiday were fairly reasonable and unlike most requests it wasn't to avoid paying the inflated prices during the school holidays either, although I agree wholeheartedly with parents who do it to save money.

Apart from the fact that we couldn't go away in the summer holidays because I was going to be working away then, another reason for asking to take our son, Cameron, out of school at the end of June to go on holiday was because my other son Josh, our eldest, was attending school during the half term holidays at the *beginning* of June which they'd opened for year 11's to study for their exams that were coming up and it was important that he studied for them. If he *hadn't* have been studying for his exams we would have gone away then, but obviously we couldn't. And we couldn't go away in the summer either. I thought our request was a reasonable one and coupled with the fact that Cameron's attendance was 98% I honestly thought they'd authorise it. I thought wrong.

It's annoying enough being issued with a penalty notice but it's even more annoying because they aren't issued fairly and across the board. For example you could be the most responsible parent in the world who makes sure your child goes to school every day. And your child could have a 100% attendance record. But if you take them out of school to go on holiday for a week you'll be issued with a penalty notice. However if a kid is absent on a regular basis, ducking school, playing truant etc and has an awful attendance record, for arguments sake say 85%, and the parents don't really give a toss, those parents won't automatically be issued with a penalty notice. So your child could be the model pupil and you could be model parents but if you take them out of school to go on holiday you'll be fined. You could also end up being treated like a criminal and hauled before the courts. Yet some other kid could be a right little shit - with equally shit parents - who *don't give a shit* about their kid attending school but they won't get issued with a penalty notice and fined straight away, they'll just get a warning.

Education penalty notices can be issued when ten unauthorised absences have been recorded in a three month period. However in most circumstances a formal warning is given first and if the kid's attendance doesn't improve a penalty notice *might* be issued. But that doesn't apply if you take your child out of school for a week to go on holiday which is classed as 10 absences (x2 a day, morning absence and afternoon absence) and if you do you'll be issued with one straight away without a warning. Now how can that be fair? You bring your kids up the best you can. You teach them right from wrong and you make sure they go to school every day, even when they might not be feeling too well. Yet take them out of school for a week to go on holiday and you'll get a fine. Yet there are parents who couldn't give a damn about their kids education and who let their kids get away with murder and they really couldn't care less if their kids are in school or not, yet they don't get fined. They're more likely to get 'guidance' than they are fined. It's a joke, but not a very funny one, and most parents aren't laughing. But at the end of the day even if you do get fined for taking your kids out of school you're still saving money as it's a hell of a lot cheaper than going away during the school holidays, which brings me to the (fairly obvious) reason why parents take their kids out of school in the first place.

As we all know, greedy holiday companies and airlines hike their prices during the school holidays. They deny it of course and say it's the other way around and that the school holiday price is the 'normal' price and at other times of the year they lower it. But that's a load of bollocks. And not only do they hike their prices during the school holidays, if the holidays or seats on a plane are selling well they'll hike them even more!

They say it's 'supply and demand' but EVERYTHING is supply and demand. Food, clothes, petrol, cars, houses, etc, etc. The list is endless. You name it. Every single thing is supply and demand. The demand is there so suppliers supply it. Yet NEVER do you see such astronomical price increases as you do in the holiday business, in particular with airlines, just because something is in demand. A couple of years ago we were thinking of going away at half term and six weeks before the departure date the return flight was £39. For one reason or another we didn't end up going but out of curiosity I kept an eye on the price and it steadily increased. And two days before departure it said there was only four seats left and the price had increased to £329! That's a 750% increase. How the fucking hell are they allowed to get away with it? Can you imagine what would happen if say Tesco's did the same thing and when you went in there on a Monday morning the shelves were full of loaves of bread priced at eighty pence each and when you went back in on the Friday there was only four loaves left and they were charging fifty quid each for them? There'd be uproar. They wouldn't be allowed to get away with it. So why are airlines and holiday companies allowed to get away with it? It's greed. Pure and utter fucking greed and that's why parents take their kids out of school during term time so they don't get ripped off. And until something is done about it to stop them ripping us off, parents will continue to take their kids out of school. And not content with hiking prices by scandalous amounts during the school holidays, airlines and holiday companies like to rip us off even more by classing some of our kids as adults.

You're not an adult until you're eighteen, simple as. So how can a twelve year old kid that goes to school be classed as an adult? They're NOT adults. A twelve year old is a child. Yet when you book a 'flight only' (as opposed to a package holiday) they're classed as an adult and you have to pay the adult fare for them. It's wrong and it shouldn't be allowed and it's just another way of making more money out of parents. And how is it that on a 'flight only' a twelve year old is classed as an adult but if you book a package holiday they're still classed as kids until they're seventeen? So effectively, two families could be sat in seats next to each other on the same row on the same plane going to the same destination with the same travel company and both families could have a twelve year old with them. And if one family has booked a 'flight only' their twelve year old would be classed as an adult and charged the adult price. Yet the other family could have booked a package holiday and *their* twelve year old would be classed as a child and they'd pay the child price - and they're sat right next to each other! It's an absolute con.

Just to prove a point, when we were once flying to Majorca having booked 'flight only', when the stewardesses came around asking if anyone wanted a drink I ordered a can of Stella and as she passed it to me I said, "Oh, and can I have a Vodka and coke for my son please," and gestured towards Cameron who was sat across the aisle with my wife. Not surprisingly the stewardess looked slightly perplexed that I was trying to buy a vodka and coke for a young kid and she said, "I'm sorry, I can't serve your son with alcohol." I asked her why not and said that Cameron was an adult - and she looked *even more* perplexed! And with a puzzled look she said, "He's an adult? How old is he?" So I said, "He's twelve," to which she replied in a snobby condescending tone, "Well he's not an adult then is he?" And so I said to her, "Well why the fucking hell have I been charged the adult price for him then?!"

If she wouldn't have been so snotty I wouldn't have said it in the manner, or used the language I did, although the stewardess at the other end of the trolley did smirk when she heard what I said. And she later came up to me and said it was a valid point that I'd made. She also agreed that the stewardess was a bit of a snotty cow.

It really is a rip off and unfortunately there's not a great deal we can do about it. Likewise, there's not a great deal we can do about being fined for taking our kids out of school to *avoid* being ripped off.

There's also one other thing that I find quite annoying. And that's how schools will freely authorise absence on the grounds of religious observance and similar religious reasons without question, whereas they won't grant it for most other reasons. They really need to look into this because it's being abused, big time, and the authorities *know* it is. Most of those parents who use this as a reason to take their kids out of school are just using it as an excuse to go on a normal holiday that entails nothing about religion, although if those parents can get away with it, and I know one or two who do it, then good luck to them. But it comes across as though schools and local councils are scared of issuing penalty notices in these circumstances for fear of being accused of discrimination. But if they're going to issue them then they should issue them across the board, to EVERYONE, and in equal measures. Though like all parents I don't think they should be issued at all. In actual fact it's probably pointless them issuing them anyway as by all accounts it isn't deterring parents from taking their kids out of school, and I read that there has been a 96% increase in parents doing it, and altogether over a quarter of a million penalty notices have now been issued nationwide. But seeing as how they *are* going to continue issuing them to us if we take our kids out of school during term time I think it's only fair that something should also be done to prevent schools from closing during term time when it suits them - even if it's just for half a day to give them time to *prepare* for parents evening and which is just a matter of putting a few tables and chairs out (Which they probably get the kids who've volunteered to stay behind and help to do while the teachers sit on their arses in the staff room.)

Horse name

Double The Heartache

Owner

Julian

Story behind the name

When I was thirteen I came home from school one day and my dad was already home. He'd finished work early and he was sat in the chair in the living room and he seemed his normal self. He asked how my day at school had been and we chatted like we normally do. He then asked me if I'd go to the florists and get some flowers for my mum for him to give her. I said I would and he gave me £20 and he told me to get the florist to make up a nice bouquet.

That was the only thing I thought odd as I'd never remembered him buying flowers out of the blue for my mum like that before. He never bought her flowers at all actually. Even on her birthday and on Valentine's Day he didn't buy her any. He'd always get her a present and a card but never flowers.

So I went to the florists which was on the high street at the top of the road and got a bouquet of flowers and then went back home. I'd been gone no more than half an hour.

We used to live in a terraced house. It was the type that when you opened the front door it had a short hallway and the stairs were directly in front of you. I put my key in the door and opened it and when I walked in and looked up at the top of the stairs I saw my dad hanging from the loft hatch with a rope around his neck.

At first I thought he was playing some kind of joke on me and I said, "Dad," in a sort of jokey tone. But then the realism hit me and I knew he wasn't playing a joke.

I dropped the flowers and ran up the stairs and when I saw his face I knew straight away he was dead. I screamed, "Dad! Dad!" and ran back down the stairs and went and banged on next doors, and I remember the look on my neighbours face when she opened it and I said to her, "My Dad's hung himself." She looked stunned and said, "What?" and she shouted to her husband, and when her husband came to the door she told me to wait there and they both went into my house. I heard her say, "Oh my god," and she came running back and called an ambulance and I burst into tears.

My mum was absolutely distraught when she came home and was told what had happened and she became even more distraught when she saw the flowers.

To this day I still have no idea why he did it. There were no financial troubles. Both my mum and dad were working. They weren't going through problems with their marriage or anything like that, everything was fine. And my dad wasn't suffering from depression or had any worries, at least not what we were aware of anyway. Something must have just clicked in his head that made him do it. The only thing that bothered me and that I couldn't get my head around, and I still can't, was the fact that he knew I was going to come back and find him like that and for a couple of years after it happened I hated him for it.

I kept asking myself why would he have wanted to do that to me? What kind of dad would send his own son to the shop to buy flowers for his mum knowing that when I walked back in I'd find him hanging there, dead? What had I done so bad to make him want to do such a thing to me? My mum said that he mustn't have been thinking straight and that he wouldn't have done it deliberately or planned it. Eventually I realised that, and accepted that there must have been something not quite right in his head that made him do it.

It affected me badly for several years but in time I came to terms with it and then twenty five years later I had to come to terms with it again when my best friend did more or less the same thing to me.

Paul had recently been to his cousin's funeral, who, like my dad had committed suicide. His cousin had a young son, though fortunately his son didn't find his dad dead like I did mine as he'd killed himself in his car by taking an overdose several miles away from where they lived.

It'd been a couple of weeks since the funeral and a few of us were having a drink in our local and Paul was saying how he thought it was selfish of his cousin doing what he did when he had a young son. Paul had a young son himself who'd just turned ten although he didn't live with him as he and his wife were separated. He also knew the same thing had happened to me and he said that it was selfish of my dad too. I said that I also thought it's a selfish thing to do but that there must be something mentally going on in some people's minds to make them want to do it. We discussed it a bit more before the conversation changed to a lighter subject and nothing more was mentioned of it.

At the end of the night as we were leaving I said to Paul that I'd call at his house in the morning on the way to work to pick up a drill that I'd lent him as I needed it the following day and he said that he'd leave it in the garage as he'd have already left for work himself by the time I got there.

The following morning when I arrived at his house I noticed his van was still on the drive and I thought perhaps he'd overslept. The curtains were still drawn too so I knocked on his front door to wake him up. I then went to the garage to get my drill and when I opened the garage door I saw Paul hanging from one of the struts in the ceiling with a rope around his neck.

It was déjà vu with my dad. I couldn't believe it. It was exactly the same. My dad knew that I'd come home and find him hanging from the loft and Paul knew that I'd be the one who found him because he knew I'd be going into the garage to get my drill. And similar to my dad who when I first came in from school seemed to be his normal self, when I was with Paul the night before he too seemed to be his normal self and there was nothing about his demeanour to suggest anything was wrong or that he was suicidal. Even more baffling was the fact that Paul was quite annoyed about his cousin 'selfishly killing himself' as he put it and leaving his son behind, and then he went and did the same thing and left his *own* son behind.

It just goes to show that even though somebody may *appear* to be in a sound state of mind you never know what thoughts might actually be *going through* their mind. Perhaps that's why there's been such a big thing made about men's mental health in recent years. And maybe if we'd have been more aware of mental health years ago my dad's, Paul's, his cousin's and many other suicides could have been prevented.

Horse name

An Upside Down World

Owner

Claire

Story behind the name

Some people get sacked for being persistently late. Some people get sacked for bad workmanship. And others get the chop if they step out of line when they're on their final warning. But how would you feel if you got the sack for putting an asparagus upside down on someone's plate?

Well as unbelievable as it may sound that's exactly what happened to one girl who was working for a billionaire who insisted that each portion of his food is placed in a certain way on his plate.

My business involves providing staff to, and catering for, the mega rich, and you would not believe the expectations and demands of some of them. The incident where the girl who was sacked for putting asparagus upside down on one billionaire's plate was extreme to say the least, by anyone's standards. And most fabulously rich people's expectations and demands are nowhere near as high, or as ridiculous, as that.

It happened at his holiday home in Saint Tropez and as the girl, or servant, as he refers to all his staff as, put the plate on the table in front of him he pointed to the asparagus and said, "Who put that on there?" And when the girl replied 'I did' he said, "They're upside down. The tips should be pointing to the bottom of the plate not the top." He then looked at his butler and calmly said, "Get rid of her." And the butler did. There and then.

But that's what some of them are like. Everything has to be just so and they're meticulous about every single thing, right down to how their food is laid out on their plate. Even the Queen has her cutlery measured with a ruler or a gauge when it's laid out on the table prior to a banquet. And the knives, forks, glasses and plates all have be exactly the same distance from the edge of the table. And no doubt the food is placed on each plate with the same precision. And it's the same with the super rich. They're paying top dollar so everything has to be exactly as they like it no matter how ridiculous it may seem to you or I. But to be fair, although this billionaire had some absolutely ludicrous demands and he spoke to his staff in not the most pleasant of manners, he never once questioned the invoice or quibbled when it came to paying. He just paid it.

Some of his demands really were ludicrous. Like where he'd have his carpets replaced as soon as the 'new smell' of them went. New carpets have a certain smell to them when they're first fitted. It's a hard smell to describe but if you've ever had a new carpet fitted, which most people have, you'll know the smell I mean.

The smell of new carpets only tends to last for a few weeks and so as soon as the smell went he'd replace the carpets. And it wasn't some cheap cord that you can pick up at Carpet Right for £3.99 a square metre either. It was more like £75 per square metre from Harrods.

His house in Mayfair was just one of around six or seven houses he owned in different places around the world. And as well as this one and his holiday home in Saint Tropez he also had houses in New York, Dubai, Paris, Switzerland and Barbados. He only spent around four months of the year, if that, at his house in Mayfair, and towards the middle of December one year one of his PA's called me and said that he and his family were thinking of staying there for Christmas and could I arrange for decorations and a tree to be put up with a few presents under it 'just in case' they decided to come. She also told me to stock the house up with food and drink and arrange for a chef to be there on Christmas day to cook their Christmas dinner. So I asked what kind of budget should I work to and she said that she'd speak with him and then transfer the money over and whatever she transferred would be the budget. I said okay, and then she said, "There are a couple of things he's requested though," and so I said, "What are they?" And she said, "Everything has to be bought from Harrods, including the Christmas tree. And the tree has to be positioned facing the front room window on the opposite side of the room. And it has to be exactly central with the middle of the window and dead level with the top of the frame." So I said no problem, it'll be done. I was tempted to ask if he had a preference which way up he wanted the tree, the tip of it pointing upwards towards the ceiling like everyone else has their Christmas tree or the tip pointing downwards like he likes the tips of his asparagus to be. But she probably would have guessed that I was being facetious and may not have seen the funny side, so I refrained. And three hours later she sent the money over. All fifty thousand pounds of it.

£50,000 may sound a lot to spend on a tree, decorations, food and drink and a few presents, and it *is* a lot, it's a *hell* of a lot, but believe me, you could quite easily spend it in Harrods - and get no change. And to give you an idea of just how much things cost in Harrods, even though you're probably well aware already of how expensive things are in there, the corner suite he's got in his front room which he bought from Harrods cost £65,000. The matching rug in front of it cost £3,750, and the small marble side tables that he's got either side of it cost £4,000 each. He also paid over £7,000 for the coffee table that's on the rug. His Savoir bed was £15,000, and he once spent £9,000 on a winter jacket for his young daughter. He also got her a cardigan the same day from there that was £3,900. And we spent £4,000 alone on baubles and other bits for the tree.

When it comes to spending money it really is another world that the wealthy live in.

I did everything that was asked for including buying presents for under the tree and arranging for a chef to be there on Christmas day to cook the dinner. Not to mention the fiasco we had with the tree.

The ceilings in his house were nearly 14ft high and the top of the window frame was 12ft but the tree was only 8ft so we had to build it up by another 4ft so that it was level with the top of the frame as he wanted it. And because he was such a perfectionist we had to make it look like it was one continuous piece of wood from where we'd joined it near the base. We then had to use a horizontal laser level to make sure the top of it was dead level with the top of the frame. Finally, we decorated it with over £4,000 worth of decorations and we put similarly expensive presents underneath it. And after doing all that he didn't turn up. His PA rang me on Christmas Eve to say that he and his family were spending Christmas in New York instead.

When you think of the poverty in this world and the amount of people who struggle at Christmas to buy presents for their kids, even though very wealthy people like him can afford it, it really is obscene to spend, or rather waste, that amount of money.

He's no longer a client of mine. For whatever reasons he chose not to use our services anymore. After we parted company he and his wife got divorced and as part of his wife's settlement she was awarded a £70,000 a year handbag allowance. Ridiculous I know, but believe it or not these types of allowances are not unusual. They're based on the lifestyle the spouse has been accustomed too and as she was accustomed to spending £70,000 a year on handbags she was awarded it. And this was on top of the several million she'd already been awarded.

I was actually called to the court hearing as a witness to back up her claim for the handbag allowance. The reason being I'd once bought seven Gucci handbags for her on her husband's instruction which cost over £9,000 each and I was asked to provide a copy of the invoice, which I did. This apparently was enough to substantiate her claim for the allowance and she was awarded it. The seven handbags I bought were all the same. They were identical. But his wife wanted seven of them so she could keep one in each of their seven houses so that she didn't have to carry the same one around with her from place to place.

And I always thought that's what handbags were for, to carry around with you? Silly me.

It does make you wonder though. What some people spend on decorating their house at Christmas and on replacing carpets and buying handbags, others could live on the same amount for many a year - and without making a fuss if their vegetables get served upside down.

Horse name

Poppycock Or Not?

Owner

Valerie

Story behind the name

I've read about dogs having a sixth sense and how they can sense danger and how they know when something bad is going to happen but I never believed it to be true. But after experiencing something with my own dogs I'm now of the opinion it is.

Many years ago I read a story about an owner who said that for two weeks before his dog died it continually kept looking up towards the sky as if it knew it would shortly be going to heaven. Then two weeks later it died of heart failure. I thought, 'poppycock', how on earth could a dog know it was going to die, it can't. And why would it look to heaven? Dogs don't go to heaven do they.

And I read another story of how when one owner was walking his dog down the road it kept pulling him towards the kerb as though it was trying to get him to cross over. The owner just carried on walking on the side of the road they were on but because his dog persistently kept pulling him towards the kerb he eventually crossed over. And as he got to the other side of the road a car came speeding around the corner and mounted the pavement on the side they'd just crossed over from and smashed into a wall. The owner said afterwards that it was as if his dog had sensed what was about to happen and made him cross over, and saved his life.

I thought both of these stories, and other similar stories I'd read, were nonsense. Well, maybe not nonsense but just coincidence. But then one day something happened that made me think that stories like these might not just be coincidence and that dogs actually can sense when something bad is going to happen.

I've always had a dog though when this happened my husband and I had *three* dogs.

My husband worked shifts in a local factory and he used to go to work on his motorcycle and whenever he left for work the dogs would just carry on doing whatever it was they were doing, which was usually just lying on the rug in front of the fire, and they wouldn't make a fuss about him leaving.

This particular week he was on a '2 - 10' shift, two o'clock in the afternoon until ten o'clock at night, and he was always back home by half past ten. And in the afternoon as he was leaving for work the dogs seemed unusually agitated and they were barking and jumping up at him and making a right fuss of him. And as he went to leave the house they ran to the front door and again kept jumping up at him as if they didn't want him to leave. It was as if they were trying to stop him from going out. So he gave them all a pat and had a bit of a play with them and then left for work. And when he closed the front door all three of them ran into the living room and jumped onto the back of the settee and looked through the window at him getting on his motorcycle. They then watched as he drove off and as he did all three of them began whimpering and once he was out of sight they went and lay back on the rug. They continued whimpering for a short while and then they stopped but for the rest of the day they were extremely quiet, and at tea time when I put their food out for them none of them ate it.

All of them were acting very peculiar.

I always used to make a sandwich for my husband for when he got in from work and later that night as I was sat watching television I looked at the clock and saw it was twenty past ten, so I got up to go into the kitchen to make it. And as I got up all three of the dogs suddenly began barking and howling at the same time. It was like nothing I'd ever heard them do before. I looked outside and then in the back garden to see if anyone was there but there wasn't. It was extremely odd, eerie even, the way they were behaving.

I thought well my husband will be back shortly and they'll settle down. But my husband didn't come back. And I never saw him again. Apart from when I had to identify his body.

I had a feeling something was wrong at around ten to eleven as he was always back at half past ten without fail. And when it got to eleven o'clock I really did start to worry. I couldn't ring him because like a lot of the older generation in those days both myself and my husband didn't have a mobile phone. We just had the house phone. So I just sat there, waiting, and worrying. And then at about half past eleven there was a knock on the door and when I opened it two policemen were stood there. That's when I knew something awful had happened.

They told me that my husband had been knocked off his motorcycle and killed on his way home from work and that he'd been pronounced dead at the scene. And at the inquest it said that the accident had happened at twenty two minutes past ten, two minutes after our dogs had started howling and barking. Was it purely coincidence - like I thought the stories I'd read about were purely coincidence - that our dogs started howling and barking at twenty past ten? Or did they sense that my husband was in danger and that something bad was about to happen to him?

Looking back on it I don't think it was a coincidence. And taking into account the way the dogs were behaving before my husband left for work that day, coupled with how they began to bark and howl two minutes before the recorded time of the accident, it seems just *too much* of a coincidence. So maybe dogs can sense danger or know when something bad is going to happen after all?

Horse name

Barbarism

Owner

Patrick

Story behind the name

Envisage being tied to a chair and forced to watch as a loved one is shot dead in front of you. Then envisage standing by their grave at their funeral and seeing them being buried and imagine how much heartache you'd be going through. And now envisage opening your front door one morning two weeks after you'd buried them and seeing their corpse propped up against a wall opposite your house. It'd be pretty horrendous wouldn't it? It'd be horrendous enough just to watch them being shot dead let alone seeing the rest of it.

Now imagine how it must feel to be forced to watch not just one loved one being shot dead in front of you but being forced to watch as every single member of your family - including your wife, kids, grandchild and your mum and dad - are shot dead in front of you, and then seeing ALL their corpses propped up against a wall opposite your house when you open your front door one morning. Well one poor guy doesn't *have* to imagine how that would feel. He *knows* how it feels, because it happened to him. And it's the kind of thing that happens when you cross the Mexican drug cartels.

I'm a freelance journalist and I mainly report on crime and drug related stories both here in the UK and abroad. And one place

I've reported on many times is Mexico and the ongoing feuds between rival cartels and gangs for the control and supply of drugs.

Some parts of Mexico where the cartels operate have some of the highest murder rates in the world and in some cities there are more drug related killings than there are soldiers killed in some wars. But it's not just the amount of murders that are shocking it's the way they are carried out, and over the years the way people have been murdered has become increasingly more shocking. Shocking isn't the right word to use anymore actually, heinous and barbaric are more appropriate words to use.

There seems to be a culture amongst the cartels and gangs to try and outdo each other in the manner they kill someone and it's almost as if there's some kind of competition to see who can carry out a murder in the most gruesome fashion. The most 'popular' way to do it at present, and has been for some time now, is to dismember the person whilst they're still alive. Gone are the days when a bullet to the head will suffice, though that still happens regularly on a daily basis. Now they cut body parts off their rivals and lay them by their side and leave them to bleed to death. Usually all that's left of them is just their torso and head. Though some go a step further and pull their victims heart out too - whilst they're still alive.

They also film it and put it on social media. One such video was doing the rounds on WhatsApp not so long ago. In that one, two of them held their victim down whilst another cut his left leg off just beneath his knee. He then showed it to him and put it on the ground next to him. They then did the same to his right leg. And when they'd cut that off they cut off both his arms. They then returned to his legs and chopped them both off at the top of his thighs. All that was left of him was the upper part of his body from his hips to his head but he was still alive, though not for long. Because they then stuck a dagger into his chest and ripped it open and pulled his heart out with their bare hands. They then posted the video online. It was as though they were taunting their rivals and saying "beat that".

Another common one they often do which you may have seen (edited) pictures of in the newspapers is where they'll murder half a dozen people at once, mutilate their bodies, put a noose around their necks and leave them all hanging from a motorway bridge so passing motorists can see them.

I also once reported on the murder of a five year old boy who was kidnapped and after the kidnappers heard that his family had been to the police they killed him by injecting battery acid into his heart and then buried his body in nearby mountains. But as shocking as that was, for me, the most shocking murder(s) I've ever reported on was the one where the man's entire family was shot dead in front of him.

He'd apparently crossed the cartels and so they went to his house where he lived with all his family. Unlike in this country, and most other countries, where the family home consists of the mother, the father and their children, it's not uncommon in places like Mexico for all members of the same family to live together under one roof. So not only will there be the mother the father and a couple of children, there may also be the grandparents and grandchildren and even aunts and uncles.

This man lived with his wife, his two teenage sons, his eleven year old daughter, another daughter who was in her early twenties who had her *own* daughter who was two years old, which was his granddaughter, as well as his own parents. There were eight family members altogether, nine including him. And two gunmen burst in, tied him to a chair and lined all his family up against the wall.

At first he thought they were going to kill *him,* in front of his family, as they had guns held to his head. But they turned the guns on his family instead and shot them all dead as he sat there helpless tied to the chair. And for good measure as they lay dead on the floor the gunmen stood over them and shot each one of them in the head, including his two year old granddaughter.

Seeing every member of his family shot dead in front of his eyes must have been abominable. The trauma and agony he must have gone through is unimaginable. You'd want to die yourself. What would be the point of living? You'd be begging for them to kill you too. But they didn't kill him. They left. Leaving him tied to the chair looking at his dead family for hours until someone turned up at his house. How sadistic is that?

He then had to go through yet more trauma and agony as he watched them all being buried at their funerals. But his agony didn't end there. His most traumatic experience was still to come. Because two weeks after he'd buried every single member of his family he opened his front door one morning to see the corpses of them all sat in a line facing his house. Those responsible for killing them had dug them up from their graves and left them propped up in a seated position against the wall opposite for him to see as soon as he walked out of his door. It would've been harrowing enough for him to have witnessed all his family being shot dead but to then see their rotting corpses sat outside his house two weeks later must have been ghastly for him.

To do something like that is abhorrent and whatever it was he'd done, which was probably very little, it certainly didn't warrant committing an act like that. *Nothing* could warrant committing such an act and I doubt very much I'll report on anything as appalling as that again.

Horse name

Ungrateful Little Bastard!

Owner

Alec

Story behind the name

When my kids were younger I always loved surprising them. The look on their faces when they realised whatever it was I'd done was brilliant and I've got some great memories of the moments when I did it. But sometimes you don't always get the reaction you were hoping for when you surprise your kids and their reaction can leave you feeling a little bit deflated. One surprise I did springs to mind and my son's reaction, or lack of it, certainly did leave me feeling a little deflated. But something else he did, or rather said, the next day, didn't only make me feel deflated it also made me think why the hell did I bother.

A group of us, some friends of ours and their and our kids, booked to go to Disney World in Florida but we didn't tell the kids we were going there. Instead, we told them we were going to Majorca and we planned to tell them at the airport where it was we were really going. There were seven kids in total. We only had the one, Jack, and he was six at the time and on the day we all got a mini-bus to the airport, and on the way we asked the kids if they were excited about going to Majorca and they all said that they were and that they couldn't wait to get there and jump in the pool. I was even more excited than them because I couldn't wait to get to the airport and tell Jack where we were really going.

When we arrived at the airport we looked for the check-in desk to Florida and we all went and stood in it. We didn't say anything at first and then Angela, one of the mums, said to the kids, "We're in the right queue aren't we kids?" and looked up at the board above the check-in desk. The kids all then looked at the board and her daughter said, "No mummy, we're not. This is the queue for Florida not Majorca. Look, it says Florida," and pointed at the electronic board above the check-in desk. And Angela said, "Well we're in the right queue then aren't we because we're not really going to Majorca, we're going to Disney World!"

We should've had our camera's out at the ready (back then mobile's weren't around so much and the ones that were didn't have cameras) because all the kids faces really were a picture.

They were even more excited about going on holiday than they already were now that they knew where they were really going, and all the kids were jumping up and down and hugging the parents and saying thanks and what have you. All the kids except one that is – Jack. He just stood there with a face like thunder and said, "I don't want to go to Florida. I want to go to Majorca." I couldn't believe it. The holiday of a lifetime and he didn't want to bleeding go!

You name it I tried it to convince him how good it was going to be, and I got the brochure out to show him, but he was having none of it. He just sulked because he wasn't going to Majorca. And when we got to the check-in desk and the girl asked him if he was excited about going to Disney World he just looked up at her and said loudly, "NO. I'M NOT!"

My wife said that once we got there he'd be totally different, but he wasn't, and after we'd spent the first day in The Magic Kingdom Park, which I thought was absolutely brilliant, as we were leaving, in a sort of exaggerated excitable tone like you sometimes speak to kids to gee them up, I said to him, "Well what did you think of that then Son!" And he replied, "RUBBISH!!!"

I couldn't believe my ears, and I stopped dead in my tracks and looked down at him and said, "You what?" and he said, "It was rubbish. The Pleasure Beach at Blackpool is better," and walked off!

I was dumbfounded. The fucking Pleasure Beach? In Blackpool? He was on the holiday of a lifetime, a holiday that some kids can only dream of and will probably never get to go on, and it'd cost me just shy of six grand and he'd rather be in bastard Blackpool, half an hour from where we lived.

I was lost for words. I just didn't know what to say. I just felt like packing our bags and going home. It really did piss me off. Though one of the other dads who heard what Jack had said thought it was as funny as fuck and was stood there laughing his bollocks off.

It's funny now. I saw the funny side a couple of days later to be honest. Actually, I saw the funny side a couple of *hours* later when me and my wife were sat there having a drink and laughing about it with the other mums and dads, but at the time I was far from amused and thought 'why bother?' But we do bother because that's what we're there for, to do the best for our kids and give them nice things - even if the ungrateful little bastards do throw it back in our faces from time to time!

Horse name

Dropping Dad In It

Owner

Billy

Story behind the name

I was driving down the road the other day with my wife and my two kids and there was a bin lorry in front of us and all of a sudden this huge dildo fell out of the back of it and bounced off the windscreen and the kids shouted, "WOW! What was that Dad?" Embarrassed, and not wanting to tell them what it really was, I said, "It was just a flying insect." To which my youngest replied, "Was it? I'm surprised it could get off the fucking ground with a cock that big!"

Obviously that was just a joke. I wasn't really driving down the road with my wife and kids and a huge dildo fell out of the back of a bin lorry and bounced off the windscreen, and my youngest didn't say that either. Though knowing *my* youngest if we ever were driving down the road and a huge dildo bounced off the windscreen and I told her it was a flying insect she probably would come out with something like that! But that's kids for you. They just say things as they see them. And I remember when one kid said something exactly how *she* saw it.

I've got quite big ears and when I was younger I always got the mickey taken out of me by other kids and I must have been called 'Big Ears' fifty times a day at school.

It still happened after I left school and I even get referred to as big ears now by one or two people I know and I'm 56! And sometimes when I'm out, say in a supermarket, young kids who are with their mum will stare and giggle but rarely do they say anything. But on one occasion a kid did say something to me but it was what she said afterwards to someone else that was even funnier than what she said to me, although her dad must have wanted a hole to open up in the ground and swallow him when she said it to the person.

It was quite a few years ago and I was on a bus. It was the older type buses that when you got on them there were two long seats first of all that sat about five people on each that ran underneath the window opposite each other at the front. You then had the seats on either side that sat two on each and ran to the back of the bus with the aisle in between.

The bus was full and nearly all the seats were taken and I was sat on one of the longer seats at the front and sat opposite me was a little girl with her dad. She was only about four or five years old and she kept staring at me. Or to be exact, she kept staring at my ears. Then all of a sudden she blurted out, "You've got massive ears!" So I started laughing and said, "Yes, I know I have!" But her dad wasn't so amused and he apologised to me and then told his daughter off and said to her, "You shouldn't say things like that." And she just replied, "Well he has!"

Her dad was an ordinary type fella. He was in his early forties maybe and he came across as a pleasant, polite, inoffensive sort of person who kept himself to himself and wouldn't harm a fly, totally the opposite of the guy who got on a few stops later.

The bus stopped and when this guy got on you could tell that everyone was thinking the same thing, "please don't sit next to me!"

He looked a right thug. And he was big too. He was that big the bus nearly tilted to one side when he got on! He was a bodybuilder and he was wearing a T shirt and a pair of knee length shorts. His arms were twice the size of my thighs and they were covered in tattoos. He was full of them, and as well as having tattoos on his arms he also had them on his neck and on his calves and shins.

After he'd got his ticket and started to walk up the bus everyone looked away from him so as not to catch his eye. He really did look like the sort that would say "what are *you* looking at?" and start trouble for no reason. The only person not to look away from him though was the little girl. She just stared at him.

As he came up the aisle the fellow next to me got up and as he did he quietly said to me, "Thank god for that. It's my stop!" And he walked down to the front of the bus to get off and as he did the tattooed terror sat in his place, right next to *me*, and right opposite the little girl. I glanced at her dad, who was doing his best not to make eye contact with the guy and it was as though he was thinking to himself about his daughter, 'I hope she doesn't say anything!' I then looked at his daughter and she had her eyes glued on the bloke, staring at him. And after looking at him for about a minute she said to him, "My Dad said that only morons have tattoos."

Oops! I thought to myself!

The guy looked at her and then glared at her dad, and with his eyes fixed firmly on him he replied, "Does he now?" and the little girl said, "Yes, he does. And he said that anyone who gets one done must be really stupid!"

All those sat near the front heard what she said and everyone that did was dying to laugh, everyone that is apart from the little girl's dad who stood up and said to her, "Right, come on. We're getting off. This is our stop." And his daughter said, "No it isn't. We never get off here. It's nowhere near home." It clearly wasn't their stop but her dad just pressed the bell anyway for the bus to stop because he wanted to get off it before the tattooed terror smashed his face in! And after he'd pressed the bell he grabbed his daughter by the arm and dragged her to the front of the bus and said to the driver, "Anywhere along here will do fine driver!"

It was one of those 'you had to be there' moments to appreciate it fully, but take 'Big Ears' word for it, it was a very funny - and awkward - moment indeed!

Another awkward moment happened to me not so long ago when I was stood in the living room one day and my son came home from school unexpectedly and walked in and asked me if he could ask me a question, so I said, "Of course you can Son what is it?" And he said, "Well, it's a bit embarrassing really and I feel a bit awkward asking you it." So I said to him, "Look, I'm your Dad. You can ask me whatever you want, now fire away." So he said, "Why have you got your knob in the Hoover?"

That was a joke too by the way!

Horse name

Tight Arsed Santa

Owner

Katrina

Story behind the name

My son believed in Father Christmas longer that most children do. A lot of kids stop believing in him when they get to about seven years old but Liam, my son, still believed in him when he was nearly nine.

It's nice that your kids still believe in Father Christmas as they get older but one problem is, as any parent will tell you, is that the older your kids get the harder it becomes to know what to get them. And not only is it harder to know what to get them as they get older, things tend to be more expensive too.

Liam had just turned nine at the time. We'd decided on what we were going to get him, and amongst other things they included an X box, with extra games for it, football boots, trainers (Nike one's) a remote control helicopter, which was nearly £200 on its own, and an iPhone.

So once we'd got everything we wrapped it all up and when he was in bed on Christmas Eve we put it all under the tree. The presents didn't look as big as they had done in previous years. When he was younger and we used to get him toys and games for Christmas they used to come in big boxes and the pile would be halfway up the tree. But even though these presents cost far more than the presents we'd bought him in the past there didn't look to be as many.

On Christmas Day Liam came bounding in our bedroom at half past five in the morning all excited like he usually is and he asked could he go downstairs to see if Santa had been. So I said, "Yes, go and see if he's been," and he ran downstairs and into the living room.

We could hear him rummaging around and picking the presents up wondering what was inside them so I shouted down to him, "Has he been?" And he shouted back, "Yes, he's been. He's not left a lot, but he's been!!"

Me and my husband looked at each other not quite believing what we'd just heard him say. It didn't look a lot compared to previous years I must admit but it'd still cost us over £600!

Horse name

A Wee Map Of Africa

Owner

Jason

Story behind the name

No matter what the weather I always wear shorts. Rain, sleet, snow, freezing cold, you name it, year 'round, I'll have them on. And one day in the middle of February when it was knee deep in snow and absolutely freezing, I had a dental appointment.

As I was sat in the waiting room, which was packed, I needed to go to the toilet so I got up and went, and as I was halfway through having a piss I heard the receptionist call out my name so I hurriedly finished it off, gave it one last squirt, and tucked myself away and came out. I then went into the dentist's room and lay on the chair.

The dentist, who was a woman, then went about checking my teeth and as she did I noticed that every now and then she kept glancing down towards my groin. I panicked at first and thought that I might not have zipped myself up properly when I'd hurried after hearing my name being called and that my cock had popped out and that was what she was staring at! But then I remembered that I was wearing my gym shorts and that they didn't have a fly or a zip, and so I just thought that the dentist must have been looking at my shorts thinking, "Why the hell is this idiot wearing shorts when it's minus ten outside and there's 2ft of snow on the ground!"

So I thought no more of it and when she'd finished I got up out of the chair and the dentist's assistant handed me my notes to give back to the receptionist. And as she did I saw that both the assistant and the dentist glanced down at my groin area again. So I took the notes, said goodbye, and left the room and once I was outside I looked down at my groin. I then realised what they'd been looking at – I had the biggest piss stain in my shorts you could imagine. It was huge. It looked like I had a map of Africa imprinted on my shorts! And right then I wished I *was* in Africa rather than at the dentist's because I now had to walk back into the reception area that was full of people, including mums with their kids.

What must have happened was that when they'd called my name out, because I hadn't quite finished peeing, a bit, or rather *quite a lot* of piss, had dribbled out after I'd hurriedly tucked myself away. And because my gym shorts were made of that Lycra type material, the sort of material that when water splashes on it it spreads all over it, when I'd dribbled it had spread right across my shorts.

It wasn't too bad walking back into the reception area because I held the notes that the dental assistant had given me in front of my shorts so they covered the piss stain but once I'd given them to the receptionist I had nothing to cover it with. To make matters worse the reception desk was at the far end of the room and I now had to walk back across it to leave - in front of everyone in there - with nothing to cover the stain. So I thought the best thing to do would be that when I turned around I'd put my hands in front of me to try and cover the piss stain and walk as quickly as I could across the room hoping that nobody noticed it. But as I turned around I didn't see a young kid who'd walked up and stood right behind me with his mum waiting to give their name to the receptionist and I walked straight into him and the top of the kid's head just happened to be level with my hip. And because he was that close I didn't get chance to put my hands in front of me and he saw the massive piss stain in my shorts, and he took one look at it, stepped back, pointed at it, and at the top of his voice shouted, "Ugh! Mummy, look. That man's weed himself!" and everyone in the room looked around and stared at it.

It was the most embarrassing moment in my life and the only saving grace was that I didn't have to go back to the dentists for another six months, which was about the same length of time it took for the pee stain to dry out!

Horse name

The Gloved Hand

Owner

Lee

Story behind the name

All kids get scared at night when they go to bed. It's dark, they're on their own, and they're afraid of 'the monsters' that come out at night. So it's natural for them to be scared - it's also natural for dads to scare their kids! No-one knows why dads feel compelled to want to scare their kids it's just something we do. Mums don't do it. It's a 'dad thing'. And bedtime is the ideal time for us dads to scare our kids. However some dads, like myself, take scaring their kids to the extreme and we aren't content with just hiding behind the bedroom door and jumping out on them and saying 'Boo'. We like to go a bit further and not only *scare* our kids but absolutely petrify them, and here's a couple of things I did to one of mine when she was younger that not only petrified her it scared the shit out of her!

When I put my kids to bed at night I always make sure that the windows are shut properly and I pull the handle to check that it's locked. And one night when I did it I said to my daughter, "I better make sure that the windows are locked so that The Gloved Hand can't get in."

As my kids got older they got used to me saying it and in the end when I used to say it to them they'd just look at me and throw their eyes in the air as if to say, "Yeah, right Dad, of course there's a gloved hand," and turn over and go to sleep. But when I first started saying it to them when they were little they'd always ask what 'The Gloved Hand' was and I'd make up a story about the bogey man who when he was once trying to climb through a child's bedroom window he was attacked with an axe by the kid's dad who was trying to stop him getting in and the dad chopped one of the bogey man's hands off. And I said that the police then came and took the bogey man away but the hand crawled off by itself, and now, at night-time, it comes out wearing a black glove and tries to get in through children's bedroom windows, and that was why I always checked to make sure they were locked, so it can't get in. It's a far-fetched story I know but to a four year old, which was how old my daughter Ella was at the time and who thought bogey men existed, it was totally believable. And it planted the seed in her head for the trick I was going to play on her.

So at bedtime the following night, and with the 'gloved hand' story in the back of her mind, when Ella was in the bathroom brushing her teeth and getting ready for bed I told her that I had to nip out and that I'd come and check on her later when I got back and I gave her a little kiss and said, "See you later." And as I walked out of the bathroom I said to her, "Don't forget to check that the bedroom window is locked so the hand can't get in," and a nervous look appeared on her face, and the gloved hand story had moved from the *back* of her mind right to the front of it. I then went downstairs and opened and shut the front door as if I'd gone out and I then went into the garage and got a pair of black gloves, that I'd purposely bought that day, and put one on and sneaked back upstairs and hid under her bed.

When Ella had finished brushing her teeth she came in the bedroom with her mum, who also thought I'd gone out, and got in bed. My wife then read her a bedtime story, said goodnight, turned the main light off and put Ella's Disney princess night light on that was on the wall by her bed and went downstairs.

I left it a few minutes and listened to Ella talking to herself, or rather listening to her talking to the princesses on her night light. I could also hear her pressing the light on and off so I knew she was facing the wall, which was perfect. So I put the back of my gloved hand against the wall and very slowly slid it up from between the side of the bed until it was level with the night light. I then paused for a couple of seconds before flopping my wrist forward so my hand fell onto her pillow. I then started moving it forward really slowly in a crawling motion.

There was a deadly silence as she stopped talking to herself and she froze, petrified, staring at 'the gloved hand that comes out at night to get kids' crawling menacingly across her pillow towards her. Then all of a sudden she let out the most ear piercing scream you could imagine followed by shouts of, "Mummy, Mummy, Mummy," who came running back up the stairs wondering what the hell had happened, and she too momentarily shit herself when she saw the gloved hand moving around on Ella's pillow! Though when she heard howls of laughter coming from under the bed it dawned on her that the hand was attached to the body of her 'childish, idiot of a husband' as she later referred to me as when telling one of her friends what I'd done. Needless to say Ella has checked under her bed ever since before getting in it at night.

Another one I did which was equally funny, and which my wife thought was equally cruel, was on Ella again.

I was putting her to bed one night and as I was tucking her in and saying 'night night,' I deliberately kept looking at the wardrobe. I don't know what it is but there's something about a wardrobe that scares kids at night. They used to scare me when I was young. I remember lying in bed in the dark and I'd try not to look at it because for some reason it frightened me and sometimes I'd convince myself that the door had opened slightly by itself and I'd hide under the duvet shitting myself. There's something eerie about wardrobes to kids. It could be the size of them or the shape of them or they might creak a bit. There's just something about them that when it's dark they make a kids imagination run wild and makes them think there's something hiding inside it. They think there's all sorts of horrible scary things lurking in there like monsters and ghosts - and one handed bogey men!

I could see from out of the corner of my eye that Ella was looking at me as I was glancing at the wardrobe and she said to me, "What are you looking at Daddy?" So I replied, "Nothing sweetheart. I just thought I saw the wardrobe door move, that's all," and I gave her a kiss, got up and walked out of the bedroom. And when I got on the landing I stopped and looked between the edge of the door and the frame and saw that Ella had pulled the bed covers right up to her chin and was staring at the wardrobe. (My wife was right. It *is* pretty cruel actually now I'm reading it!)

However, even though there were no monsters or one handed bogey men hiding in her wardrobe, my mobile phone was. And earlier that day I'd made a voice recording on it and set it as the ring tone. So I went downstairs, turned the landing light off (to make it even more scary for her) went in the living room and rang my mobile off the landline and the voice recording that I'd set as the ringtone came on.

Now imagine that you're a four year old lying in bed in the dark staring at the wardrobe - with the duvet pulled up to your chin frightened to death because your dad had just told you that he thought he'd seen the wardrobe door open by itself - and all of a sudden from inside the wardrobe in a slow, droning, spooky, haunting ghost-like voice you hear, "WOOOOOOH, WOOOOOOOOOOOOH, ELLAAA, I'M COMING TO GET YOOOOOUU ELLAAA, WOOOOOOOOOOOOH!

Well, Ella absolutely shit herself. Again! All you heard was a loud thud as both feet hit the floor as she jumped out of bed, and she came running down the stairs screaming, "Daddy, Daddy, there's something in the wardrobe and it's coming to get me!"

Ella never did nominate me for any Dad Of The Year awards, although over the years she has come close to 'nominating' me to Childline on a number of occasions!

The clock ticks fast once you have kids and the older your kids get the faster the clock ticks and it ticks faster and faster every day and time whizzes by at an alarming rate; Another birthday, gone. Another Christmas, gone (another £600 on presents, gone!) and before you know it, another year's gone. Then all of a sudden, in what seems like the blink of an eye, your kid's childhood has gone too and they're no longer kids. It zips past:

Born
Nursery
Primary School
Secondary School
Sixteen
Childhood over

It's frightening really how quickly it passes and how soon they grow up and the thought of my two growing up and not being 'daddy's little angels' anymore used to frighten me. You could say I got the 'wardrobe' feeling about it, where similar to young kids that lye in bed at night staring at their wardrobe and get scared thinking what might be in there, it used to scare me a bit thinking about Ella and Lily growing up and no longer being kids. I didn't want them to grow up, I wanted them to stay young so I could carry on acting daft with them and carry on doing all the silly things that dads do with their kids. And I didn't want the day to come when they no longer wanted to hold my hand as I walked down the street with them, although Ella has been reluctant to hold my hand for some years now ever since I hurled her into the middle of the road when she was on her roller skates and broke her arm! And I was going to miss walking them to school every morning, though Lily probably wasn't going to miss that seeing as how I once told her it was 'Silly Friday' and that I was going to walk her to school with my underpants on my head! And I was going to miss picking them up again *after* school and the teacher showing me a poem that suggested I was a homosexual! But sadly those days have come and gone and Ella and Lily are now both in their teens and I really wish I could turn the clock back to when they were young and do it all over again. It's an overused phrase but just where *did* the time go? So if you've got young kids yourself make every day with them count because take my word for it before you know it *your* fun times with *your* kids will have come and gone too and like me you'll be sat there one day wondering where the hell the time went. And so if your kids ask you to play or do something with them don't say "in a minute" and then forget. Just do it. Get off your phone, get off the computer, put the newspaper down - put this book down - and enjoy every single minute with your kids because before you know it they'll have grown up and they won't be kids anymore, and even though they'll still be your kids and you'll always love them as much as you did from the day they were born and you'll still have great times with them, those times won't *quite* be the same as the times you have with them when they're young.

Horse name

Hanging Loose

Owner

Helen

Story behind the name

Have you ever been in one of those situations where you're that embarrassed you just want the ground to open up and swallow you? Or you wish you could just click your fingers and magically disappear from the awkward position you've found yourself in? I'm sure you have. And I'm sure it was highly embarrassing for you. However whatever the embarrassing situation was that you were unfortunate enough to find yourself in I can guarantee that it would've been nowhere near as embarrassing as the situation my husband found *himself* in. It was also highly embarrassing for me too.

Three years ago my husband had a vasectomy and for a few days afterwards it was quite painful for him. It wasn't excruciating pain it was more 'tender' and a feeling of discomfort and he found that as well as taking the odd painkiller when needed, not wearing the tight fitting boxer shorts he wore helped relieve the discomfort too. So he went 'commando' and let his tackle hang loose so to speak.

The discomfort didn't prevent him from going about the everyday things that he'd normally do, including going to work. We run our own marketing company and we have a small office in London not far from Waterloo station which we commute to by train from where we live in Kingston in Surrey. And after having the 'snip' on the Wednesday he went back to work on the Thursday.

The following day, Friday, as we were about to leave the office at the end of the day I noticed that the zip on his trousers was wide open. And with him not wearing any underwear I could see virtually everything! So I told him to zip himself up but when he went to do so he found that the zip was broken. Fortunately for my husband there's only ever me and him at the office so he didn't have to worry about anyone seeing anything they ought not to. However at Waterloo station where we catch the train home from he *isn't* the only person there. There are *hundreds* of people there. And the trains are heaving with commuters. Even more so on a Friday evening. So I told him he'd need to find something to secure his zip with to make sure that nothing was on show before he left the office.

He asked me if there were any safety pins anywhere in the office to pin his fly's together with and I said there wasn't. And so in order to keep his privates private and not risk accidentally exposing himself at rush hour at one of the busiest train stations in London he stapled his fly's together with the office stapler.

It seemed like a good idea at the time but when you think about it an office stapler is only good enough for stapling and holding together around 10 sheets of A4 paper at best, let alone hold together the fly's on a pair of thick cotton trousers. And once you've stapled sheets of paper together they're usually left flat on a desk. And with them lying flat on a desk nothing causes the tiny metal staples to come loose. But when those tiny metal staples are used to hold together the fly's on a pair of men's trousers, which they're not meant for in the first place, and the man wearing the trousers starts moving around in them as opposed to lying flat on a desk, the staples are bound to come loose. And unbeknown to my husband, no sooner had he started walking when we left the office that's what happened; the staples began to loosen.

As we were walking from the office to Waterloo, every now and then I glanced down at my husband's fly's to make sure they were still together, and they looked as though they were. And when we got to Waterloo we had about a fifteen minute wait for our train so we sat on a bench on the concourse, and when it showed on the departure board that our train had arrived and was ready for boarding we got up and walked to the platform.

It didn't dawn on me or my husband at the time that the motion of bending and sitting down, which naturally causes trousers to tighten around the groin and crutch area, was obviously going to loosen the staples even more, although as we were walking to the platform, when I glanced down again at his fly's they looked like they were still together.

When we got on the train, because it was that busy we couldn't get two seats together. So my husband sat on a seat at the front facing the doors that led into the next carriage and I sat about six seats behind him. He was sat on the outside seat, the aisle seat, and so was I, and we were talking to each other as people boarded the train. The train was getting busier. And eventually, as usual, there were no seats left. So people began to stand at the front near the doors where my husband was sat and because my husband and I were talking to each other it was obvious to anyone who was sat or stood near us that we were together.

The doors of the train closed and it began to move and so we finished our conversation and my husband sat back in his seat, and about ten minutes into the journey I noticed his head had flopped to the side slightly. He'd nodded off. Which he often did on the journey home. I also noticed that one or two of the people who were stood near him had smirks on their faces. I then noticed more people around him were smirking and that one or two were laughing.

Ironically, as the people were laughing and smirking the digital display above them that listed the stations the train stopped at caught my eye. And as the stations flashed across the screen I noticed that one of them was Hampton Wick. But not for one minute did it cross my mind that the reason people were laughing and smirking was because my husband's fly's had popped open and he was flashing *his* Hampton Wick!

Out of all the people who were laughing one was laughing more than anyone else. He was absolutely wetting himself. He then gestured to me with his hand and gave a little wave as though he was trying to attract my attention. He'd obviously seen me talking to my husband a few minutes earlier and knew that I was with him. And then looking directly at me he said loudly, "Excuse me. Do you know your husband's fly's are undone and half his cock's hanging out!" and pointed down at my husband.

Virtually everyone in the carriage burst out laughing and all those who were sat and stood in the vicinity of my snoozing husband turned and looked at him. Or rather, they turned and looked down at his fly's.

I really did just want a hole to open up and swallow me - or just drop me out of the floor of the train onto the tracks below! I thought, "Oh my god! No!" And I got out of my seat and walked to where my husband was sat. And sure enough it *was* hanging out! To say I was mortified would be understating it slightly. And when I woke him up so too was my husband. We had to get off the train at the next stop because he - and I - were that embarrassed. And the people onboard were still laughing as it pulled away again. And the guy who said what he did even gave us a little wave as the train pulled out of the station - with a big grin on his face!

Although it was extremely embarrassing at the time, by the time we got home we'd seen the funny side and were laughing about it. And I've ribbed my husband about it ever since. When he said he was going to hang loose I didn't realise he meant *that* loose!

Horse name

All That Glitters

Owner

Brendan

Story behind the name

Video doorbells, the type you see advertised on television that are linked to your phone so you can see who's calling - or prowling - around your house when you're away from home have become quite popular recently. However similar doorbell gadgets have been around for a long time, one of which is an audio bell that comes with an amplifier. It's more of a novelty type bell and you can download and record your own sounds on it and set them as the bell tone so that when someone rings the bell they'll hear it. And the idea is that you leave the amplifier near the inside of the front door, or in the porch if you have one, so it sounds really loud when someone presses the bell. And you can record things like a lion roaring, or a gorilla grunting and beating it's chest, or a grizzly bear growling, and it makes the person who rings the bell jump a bit and wonder what the hell kind of pet you keep. You can also download insulting 'welcome' messages so that when somebody presses the bell a voice rudely shouts, "What do you want!!" or "Sod Off, I'm busy!"

And after we'd bought the kids a little puppy which we called Teddy I bought one of these novelty bells after I had an idea which I thought would be funny.

Teddy was a little white fluffy thing. He was tiny and he only had a tiny little 'yap' as opposed to a bark. It was the softest pup you could imagine and it was deal for kids. It was also ideal for my little joke. So once I'd got the bell I downloaded the sound of a vicious, snarling dog barking its head off and set it as the bell tone. It sounded really vicious, like the sort of dog you'd find guarding a scrap yard such as a Rottweiler or an Alsatian, the sort that'd tear you to shreds if you stepped foot in there. And I put the amplifier above the front door and turned the volume up. I then tested it. And when I pressed the bell I nearly jumped out of my skin, and knew it wasn't real!

It sounded really life like and that there really was a big, vicious, snarling, saliva drooling dog bearing its teeth on the other side of the door. I'd also bought a 'Beware Of The Dog' sign which I put on the wall under the bell outside so people would see it. And after I'd set it all up I went back inside and waited for someone to call. And sod's law nobody did, all day!

The following morning, which was a Sunday, when I went to get something from my car, George, one of the neighbours shouted to me from across the road, "Don't answer your door," and smirked and nodded towards the end of the street. And when I looked I saw half a dozen men and women, who were all in their Sunday best and holding some kind of books, coming out of one of the other neighbour's gardens. They closed the gate behind them and went to the house next door and as they did George shouted, "Bible-Bashers!" So I said to him, "Watch them when they knock on my door!" And I went back in and got Teddy and put him in the hallway. I then made sure the volume on the amplifier was turned right up and waited behind the door. Five minutes later they all came walking down my path and after one of them had rang the bell the sound of my ferocious, snarling, rabid, throat tearing Rottweiler of a guard dog began to blast out. So I put my head to the door and shouted, "Hang on a minute. Just let me get hold of the dog. It's a right nasty bastard and it'll rip you to pieces if it gets a grip of you."

I couldn't see their reaction because our front door is a wooden one but George did and he told me later that every one of them stepped back from the door and looked really nervous. And when I shouted about it ripping them to pieces he said that one of them pointed to the 'Beware Of The Dog' sign and turned and darted back up the path looking feared to death!

I left it a couple of seconds and opened the door slightly and popped my head around it. But I only opened it a little bit so that they could only see me and not Teddy. And as they all stood there, with panic stricken faces, I said to them, "I won't be a minute, I'll just get him under control." I then stepped back behind the front door and picked Teddy up and opened the door fully so they could see him. And the Bible-Basher's faces went from panic, to relief, to confusion as they all looked at me holding what looked like a little white bunny rabbit in my arms thinking, "How the hell does that farty little thing bark like it does?"

GOD, it was funny!

I did another funny one involving Teddy as well although I didn't plan this one it was just a spur of the moment thing. But even though *I* thought it was funny the woman it involved didn't see the funny side.

Teddy really is a cute little dog and people are forever stopping me when I'm out walking with him asking if they can stroke him. And one morning when I was out with him this woman stopped me and asked could she stroke him, and so I said yes.

Like most dogs do, Teddy loves having his tummy tickled and whenever someone stops us he knows what's coming and the first thing he does is roll on his back with his legs in the air! So the woman kneels down and starts to rub his tummy. And as she's tickling and stroking him she's saying things to him like, "Oooh, aren't you lovely!" and "You're gorgeous, you are!" She then says to me, "What's he called?" So I said, "He's called Gary Glitter." And she looked at me, and with a contorted look on her face she said, "You've called your dog Gary Glitter?" And I said, "Yes - he loves playing with kids!"

She didn't find it funny!

In fact, she looked absolutely disgusted! And she stopped tickling Teddy, gave me a filthy look and got up and walked off, leaving Teddy lying on his back looking up at me thinking, "You fucking wanker! I was enjoying that!"

Horse name

Tickled Pink

Owner

Brendan

Story behind the name

I worked in Berlin in Germany for several years bricklaying and as well as earning good money it was a good laugh too. As anyone who has ever worked on building sites will tell you there's always banter and piss taking and sometimes you've got to be pretty thick skinned to take it because there are no boundaries when it comes to hurling insults or taking the piss. It can be wicked at times and rule number one, not just on building sites but in life in general, is that if you give it out you've got to be able to take it when someone gives it you back. Most can, and do, but you'll always get those who can't. They don't mind giving it out but they don't like it when someone says or does something back to them. And one person who was exactly like that was a joiner on the site called 'big Frank', and he *really was* big. He was seventeen stone and he was handy with it too and he could be a right nasty bastard when he wanted to be. He also had a very short fuse, and he was arrogant as well. In a nutshell he was a fucking arsehole! And apart from him being a fucking arrogant arsehole he also had a right hang up about gays, and I do mean a right hang up. He hated anything to do with homosexuality, so of course we played on it and wound him up about it, even though you risked getting your fucking head kicked in off him for doing so!

We'd do things like when we were walking towards him on the scaffold and it was a bit tight and there wasn't much room we'd squeeze past him but deliberately thrust our groin against the back of him and say things like, "Oh, sorry Frank. My cock just touched your arse then," and he'd spin around and grab you by the throat and scream, "FUCK OFF, right? Don't fucking do that to me."

It really wound him up.

But like I say, it was alright for *him* to take the piss and do things to us like bending our spirit levels in half or burying our trowels in the bottom of the mortar tub, but do it back and he didn't like it and he'd throw a wobbler. And I did two things to him that caused him to throw a couple of *real* wobblers. One of which was a HUMUNGOUS wobbler.

The first one was when he was fitting some soffits and facia boards on the corner of the building and I was filling in some holes near the top of the gutters. It was an awkward job as you had to lean through the scaffolding and reach around towards the gable end and there was only enough room for one person at a time. So I let Frank do his bit first and I stood behind him passing him his gear. He was leaning through the scaffolding with his back to me and he asked me to pass him his claw hammer and he reached his arm back behind him and held his hand out. But instead of putting his hammer in his hand I unzipped my fly's and got my cock out and stuck *that* in his hand instead, and he grabbed hold of it thinking it was the handle of his hammer. He realised it wasn't his hammer he had hold off and he squeezed it a couple of times trying to figure out what it was and I started laughing and said, "Instead of squeezing it Frank would you mind pulling it," and he looked back over his shoulder and down at his hand. And to his horror his worst nightmare had come true - he was holding another man's penis!

He went ballistic and he started screaming and shouting that he was going to kill me, and he wriggled back through the scaffolding, picked up his claw hammer and tried to hit me over my head with it! A few of the lads stepped in and grabbed hold of him to try and restrain him, which took some doing, and he eventually calmed down. But a few days later I did something else to him that if he'd have got hold of me not only would he have killed me he'd have torn me limb from limb.

As well as Frank being a right nasty bastard who could dish it out but couldn't take it when you gave it him back, he was also a creature of habit and every morning, religiously, at half nine he'd go for a crap, and he'd always use the same Portaloo.

There were ten Portaloos on site altogether, all side by side, but for some reason he always used the same one. Christ knows why because they were all the same. They were all blue, they were all disgusting and they all stank. And if you've ever worked on a building site, be it in Germany or in England you'll know exactly what Portaloos are like when they're used regularly by a hundred and fifty hairy arsed builders. But Frank had his preference and it was ideal for what I had planned.

One Monday afternoon before we finished for the day I made a hole about the size of a fist in the back of the Portaloo that he always used. I didn't make the hole the size of a fist because I intended fisting him if that's what you're thinking, he'd have *definitely* torn me limb from limb if I'd have done that to him! Although I had a funny feeling he wasn't going to appreciate this joke either.

I cut a piece out just below where the seat was and then taped it back on again, and the reason I did it on a Monday afternoon was because they used to empty the Portaloos on a Monday morning. I certainly wouldn't have done it on a *Friday* afternoon after they'd been used all week and were full because if I had have done the joke would have been on me. So too would've fifty litres of shit and piss!

On the Tuesday morning I told everyone what I was going to do and at half past nine on the dot Frank went into his favourite Portaloo. So I crept over behind it and pulled off the tape and removed the piece of blue plastic. And when I looked inside it wasn't a pretty sight I can tell you. But even though Frank's hairy fat arse was a fairly disgusting sight it was exactly the sight I was hoping to see, and his homophobia was quite literally going to get a grip of him. And so with all the lads stood on the scaffolding watching, and laughing, including the Germans (they have got a sense of humour despite what's said about them) I rolled my sleeve up and put my hand in the hole and reached through and started tickling Frank's balls. I then grabbed hold of them and squeezed them, twice, and shouted, "HONK, HONK" through the hole as I did it.

Tickled pink? Was he fuck! He was fucking crimson. With rage!!

I'm not exaggerating, he jumped that high off the toilet seat he banged his head on the top of the Portaloo, which was about 7ft high! And after he'd pulled his jeans up he came hurtling out, looked around the back of it - I'd disappeared sharpish and hid - and then started running around the site like a lunatic trying to find who'd done it whilst bawling, "I'LL FUCKING KILL YOU YOU CUNT. I'LL FUCKING KILL YOU!!" And I don't doubt he would have done if he'd have got hold of me. He was livid.

The lads up on the scaffolding, who were all well out of his way, were all laughing at him which made him even more livid and he started lobbing bricks at them. But they weren't reaching because they were too high up and they kept on laughing at him. So Frank got in the dumper truck and drove it into the scaffolding trying to knock them off it. He was going utterly berserk. He then reversed the dumper truck and drove it into the scaffolding again and this time the scaffolding slammed into the brickwork, and because we'd only just built it and the cement hadn't fully set, all the brickwork began to collapse. The scaffolding then started to shake and so a few of the lads jumped off it into the building. But some didn't. Then part of the scaffolding collapsed and about a dozen of them fell to the ground, a result of which six or seven of them ended up in hospital. Fortunately none of them suffered serious injury, just the odd broken arm here and there and a couple of fractured ribs between them.

None of them blamed me for what happened, even though the joke did backfire slightly, and me and my mates left the site a few days later and went working in another part of Berlin. As for Frank he didn't get chance to leave the site because the police were called as soon as he began kicking off and he got arrested. I'd loved to have been a fly on the wall down at the police station when he gave his explanation to them for reacting how he did...

"Well, it was like this officer. I was sat there having a crap when someone started tickling my balls..."

I bet the coppers pissed themselves as much as the lads on the scaffolding did!

There was another incident on the same building site that also involved a portaloo that was just as funny.

There'd been a disagreement between some Scouser's who were working on the site and the site agent, a German called Karl, over some work that had been done and Karl had docked the Scousers £200 each from their wages which they weren't too happy about. It wasn't the first time he'd done it to them either so they decided to leave and get work elsewhere, which wasn't a problem as there was tonnes of work around. You could literally walk off one site in the morning and be working on another one in the afternoon. Though more often than not if you did walk off one site in the morning you'd go straight on the piss - for several days! And get a job elsewhere the following week.

This particular day was a Friday and as the Scousers were loading their van up with tools - the majority of which didn't belong to them (that's not like the Scousers is it!) one of them noticed that Karl had gone into the Portaloo. So they ran over to it and started to rock it. And rock it. And rock it and rock it and rock it! And then they pushed it over and started to roll it around on the floor.

All you could hear from inside it was Karl shouting, "Nein! Nein! Nein!" Though personally I gave it a ten - I thought it was brilliant! Though someone *did* call 999 and half an hour later the police turned up. Again! Just like they had when Frank went mental. I bet the coppers couldn't wait for Berlin to be rebuilt so all the English could fuck off home and stop causing havoc! But unlike the day when the police turned up and found that Frank was still there, and arrested him, when they turned up *that* day they found that the Scousers had vanished. And so had all the power tools!

But what made that incident even better, or worse from Karl's point of view, was that with it being a Friday and the Portaloo's not getting emptied until Monday, it was full to the top. And not only was it completely full, it was overflowing.

Now I don't know if you've ever had the misfortune to have had to use a Portaloo when it's full to the top - and overflowing - like that one was, but if you have then you'll know just what a disgusting experience it is. And if you haven't I'll try and give you some idea of what it's like trying to use one when they're in that condition.

It's not too bad if you only need a slash because you can just stand in the pool of piss that's already there, in your work boots, and aim it in. Or you can just piss all over the floor like everyone else seems to do, which is far easier! But if you're bursting for a crap it's not so easy. You can't sit down because the seat is covered in piss, and if you *did* sit down, because it's that full you'd feel someone else's cold turd brush against your arse cheeks as it bobs along beneath you. Not only that, when a turd drops out of *your own* arse and hits the water it splashes blue dye and disinfectant - and a week's worth of eighty different blokes piss - all over your buttocks. So to avoid that you have to take your trousers down to your knees (you can't take them all the way down to your ankles like you normally would at home because if you did they'd be draping in the pools of piss that are on the floor) then bend your knees, push against the sides of the Portaloo with your hands to brace yourself, and hover about a foot over the seat and have a dump. It's a fucking nightmare! So imagine what a nightmare it must have been for Karl stuck in that position in the disgusting foul Portaloo *he* was in when the Scousers started rocking it from side to side and then pushed it over and started rolling it around. It wouldn't exactly have been a barrel of laughs for him! Though after the Scousers had done it *they* were laughing! And as they ran off some of the other

Germans ran over and lifted the Portaloo back up and Karl opened the door and came staggering out, totally disorientated, with his trousers around his knees and covered from head to toe in piss and shit, with bits of soggy bog roll stuck all over him! Naturally, Karl didn't see the funny side, though everyone else, particularly the English, thought it was fucking hilarious!

Horse name

Chop Chop We're Off To Bangkok

Owner

Billy

Story behind the name

If a wife was to find out that her husband was humping someone else she'd naturally have the hump herself and if she wasn't the forgiving type more often than not it would lead to the wife separating from the husband. When this happens most wives usually just opt for the standard separation proceedings as in using a solicitor and the divorce courts. But when some wives find out that their husband's have been shagging someone else they go for a *different kind* of separation proceedings; they go and get a large kitchen knife and proceed to separate their husband's cock from the rest of his body!

There have been many stories of wives cutting off their husband's penises after discovering they've been seeing someone else. One woman even cut her husband's penis off twice! Though probably the most well known story about a husband having his cock cut off by his wife is that of John Wayne Bobbitt who lived in America and who hit the headlines worldwide after it happened to him in the 1990's. He also made the headlines again a few years later when he went on to become a porn star after having his cock sewn back on.

Only in America as they say!

So the story goes, after he'd been out drinking all night he went home and allegedly raped his wife. He then fell asleep. And whilst he was sleeping, his wife, who in court said she'd suffered years of abuse from him, went downstairs, got an eight inch kitchen knife and went back in the bedroom and cut his knob off with it. She then got in her car, with his knob, drove off, and threw it out of the window into a field a couple of miles away. Fortunately for her husband his pecker wasn't nibbled on or eaten by the local wildlife and after his wife told the police where she'd flung it when she was arrested they recovered it in one piece.

It was successfully sewn back on and after getting divorced, and with his cock back in virtually full working order, JWB as he became known (**J**ohn **W**ayne **B**obbitt,) made a couple of porno's.

I bet he used to fucking shit himself - and grab hold of his cock with both hands - whenever the director shouted, "Cut!"

Other stories that have made the headlines about blokes having their chopper's chopped off by irate wives include one where an unfaithful husband in Peru who was fast asleep in bed not only had his chopper chopped off by his wife after she found out about his secret love life, she chopped his knackers off as well! And instead of getting in her car and driving a few miles up the road with them to throw them in a field like JWB's wife did she saved herself a journey and just took them in the back garden and poured petrol on them and set fire to them - and her husband came running out to see his love life going up in smoke. Literally! There was no chance of *him* becoming a porn star like JWB did after that! The poor fucker didn't even get to have his crown jewels sewn back on let alone make his porn debut because his cock and balls were burnt to a cinder. They'd been cremated. Right in front of his eyes! You can picture him in his back garden can't you, stood there stamping on his own cock trying to put it out!

Another woman in Taiwan did a similar thing too and cut off all of her husband's tackle whilst he was asleep in bed. But instead of pouring petrol on them and setting fire to them she poured acid on them and then flushed them down the bog!

She used a pair of garden shears to cut them off with and when she was arrested she told police she was "quite surprised how easy they came off." I bet her husband was quite surprised too when he woke up and saw his wife standing by the bed with a pair of garden shears in one hand and his knackers in the other! And a woman in China made a bit of a meal about cutting her husband's meat and two veg' off. She didn't make a meal out of cutting them off in the sense that she prolonged the ordeal in order to make her husband suffer or made a meal out of doing it as in she struggled to cut them off. She literally *did* make a meal out of his meat and two veg. And after hacking them off she boiled them in a pan of water and added them to the evening meal she was cooking on the stove.

She must have been making Coq Au Van!

Her husband had been drinking all afternoon and fell asleep blind drunk on the sofa and he didn't even know she'd done it until he woke up and went for a piss and looked down. What a shock that must have been for him. He'd have been in for another shock at tea time too when his wife put his plate in front of him at the dinner table and he saw that it had his bollocks on it! I wonder if she saved his cock for desert and made him Spotted Dick out of it! Though one woman in China wasn't satisfied with lobbing her old man's pecker off just the once, so after he'd had it reattached she *unattached* it again.

What instigated it was that her husband had used his wife's phone to send his lover a saucy email, but the dick, no pun intended (well it *was* intended actually!) forgot to log out of his account and his wife read the email - and all the other emails he'd sent to his lover - and was enraged. And later that night when he was fast asleep she got a pair of scissors and cut off the dick's dick! But she didn't throw his cock away or set fire to it or pour acid on it like the other wives did - she just left it on his stomach. Her husband woke up, in agony, saw his cock stuck in his belly button and rang an ambulance and he was rushed to hospital. And after a nine hour operation he had his knob back on. But not for long. Because a couple of days later his wife sneaked into the recovery room he was in at the hospital and cut it off again. And threw it out of the window!

Could you imagine if you were walking past on the pavement below when she threw it and it landed on your head! You'd look a right *dick head*!

So after the cheesed off Chinese lady hurled her husband's knob out of the window she ran off. And her husband, who must have been in a state of shock, not surprisingly, chased after her and caught up with her outside the hospital. And when hospital staff came running out they saw him stood over his wife knocking fuck out of her with blood pissing down his legs that was coming from a hole where his cock used to be. Unfortunately for him they couldn't find his cock and the police later said it was more than likely that a stray dog had found it and eaten it. Talk about a dog with two dicks! The dog that found it *did* have had two dicks - one between its legs and one in its mouth!

I suppose you could say that the surgeon at the hospital made a dog's dinner out of sewing that bloke's knob back on!

Those stories are one's which I've read about in the newspaper or seen on the news or on the internet, although I have personally come across one bloke who's been 'given the chop' by his wife. He also showed me what he had left of it, which wasn't much. And I wasn't the only one he showed it too. He'd show it to anybody - for twenty Baht. Around fifty pence!

It was in Bangkok (aptly named considering what the story's about!) in Thailand where I was staying for a couple of days before going on to Phuket where I was meeting a few of my mates who were already there.

It was a really good holiday that one, and apart from seeing a bloke who'd had his knob ripped off flash what was left of it at me for fifty pence, a couple of other things stick in my mind about it. One of them was a joke that I played on my mate that didn't quite go according to plan and which may well have ended with me having my own knob ripped off by an irate Norwegian fella if I hadn't have swam away from him as quick as I did. But the first thing that springs to mind whenever I think of that holiday is when I went to book it and the comment I made to the woman in the travel agents which to this day I still think was the reason I had to endure the longest long haul flight you could imagine to get there. In actual fact it wasn't a long haul flight at all it was a series of *short haul* flights that *amounted* to a long haul. *A hell of a long haul.*

Unlike now when booking a holiday or a flight, where most people do it themselves from home on a laptop or on their phone, at the time, twenty odd years ago, most people used to go to a travel agents to book their holiday. And I booked this holiday at the travel agents too.

When I went in I said to the woman who was sat behind the desk that I wanted to go to Phuket and she said, "Oh right. I'll get you a brochure for Thailand," and she indicated to the brochures that were on the top shelf across the room. She was wearing what looked like a maternity dress. She also looked like she was about to give birth any day, and as she stood up she winced and said, "Oooh!" and pulled a face as though she was in a little bit of pain. So I said, "It's okay. You sit down. I'll get it if you're pregnant." And she glared at me and said, "I'm NOT pregnant!"

Oops! How to put your foot in it with a fatty!

I tried to make amends by saying that it was her 'baggy' dress that made me think she was pregnant. But all that did was make matters worse because it was like I was insinuating she looked untidy and that she had shoddy dress sense - as well as being fat! I may as well have just walked in there and said, "Can you book me a flight to Thailand please - you scruffy fat cow!"

You know when you can feel yourself digging an even bigger hole for yourself that the one you're already in, well it was one of them kind of moments. So I jokingly said, "Well that's just put three hundred quid on the price of the holiday hasn't it!" But she didn't smile or laugh, she was obviously highly offended by my comments about her being pregnant and about her 'baggy' dress, and she just abruptly asked for the details of when I wanted to go, which I told her was as soon as possible. I also wanted to get out of the shop as soon as possible! So I didn't even bother getting the brochure off the shelf. Instead, I just asked her to try and find something for me and I left her my phone number and asked her to call me if she managed to find anything. And two hours later she rang to say she *had* found something and that it was from Manchester the following day, which was ideal. And it was cheap, which made it even better.

She didn't stick three hundred quid on the price of it after all!

So I gave her my credit card details and she said that because it was such short notice it was ticket on departure; you get your tickets at the airport. And her parting words were, "Have a nice flight." And although my comments about her being pregnant and having bad dress sense didn't put an extra £300 on the price of the holiday it did put around an extra twenty four hours on the flight. Or *flights* as it were. Because although the flight did go from Manchester, what fatty 'forgot' to mention was that it only went as far as Heathrow. I then had to get another flight from Heathrow to Schiphol airport in Amsterdam. And then from Amsterdam I had to get a flight to Zurich. I then had to fly from Zurich to Dubai, and from Dubai I had to get a flight to Hong Kong. And then from Hong Kong I had to fly to Bangkok where I had to spend two days before I could get a connecting flight to Phuket.

What a journey *that* was. I bet Michael Palin would've been proud of that one! I felt like I'd been travelling for eighty days myself by the time I got there!

It could well have been that because it was such short notice those flights were the only ones available and I did say that I wanted to go as soon as possible. Though I still think the fat cow deliberately booked all those connecting flights to get her own back on me for what I said to her!

The other thing I'll always remember about that holiday is the joke that I played on Andy, one of my mates who I met up with, that backfired, and that a bloke from Norway inadvertently ended up being the brunt of.

Thailand is great for snorkelling. It really is. Some of the fish you see are amazing. You see all sorts. And here's a tip for you the next time you go snorkelling on holiday. Take some bread and a banana (that's out of the skin) with you and scrunch it all together and drop it in front of you in the water. The fish go mad for it. You'll be surrounded by them. But don't do what I once did with it in front of a load of Japanese tourists in the sea off Phi Phi Island in Thailand when I was once snorkelling there and drop it in your swimming shorts for a laugh. That joke backfired too. My shorts were invaded by shoals of Red Snapper and it was no laughing matter having them snapping away on my nuts I can tell you! Though the Japanese tourists thought it was brilliant and they all started taking photographs with their underwater cameras!

So one day me and Andy went snorkelling in the sea in Phuket. We went down to the beach, got a couple of sunbeds, left our towels on them, put our beach bag under one of them, put our snorkelling masks on and went in the sea and swam out.

If you've ever been snorkelling you'll know that basically all you do is float along on top of the water, looking down at the fish. It's dead easy. But it's surprising how far you can drift when you're doing it. You might start off near the beach but next minute, when you look up, you could be two hundred feet away from it. Anyway, we'd been out there for about half an hour and when I looked up I saw that I'd drifted about fifty feet away from Andy. I could see his bright blonde bleached hair that he had ('streaked' hair as they used to call it back then) and he had his face in the water floating along looking at the fish, so I swam over to him. And as I got near him I whipped my shorts off, took a deep breath, went under the water, swam down about six feet and swam past underneath him naked, looking up at him waving - and waggling my knob at him - with a big grin on my face!

I came up facing the beach and when I looked over I saw someone picking up one of the towels off our sunbeds. The fucker then went underneath the sunbed and picked our beach bag up. So keeping my eye on him I half turned my head and shouted, "Andy, quick! Some thieving cunt's rifling our gear!" And I started to swim back towards the beach. All I heard from behind me was a load of coughing and spluttering and when I looked back I saw this big blonde fella spitting seawater out of his mouth. And then when I looked back towards the beach I realised that the 'thieving cunt' was Andy getting his fags out of the bag! He'd gone back about five minutes earlier whilst I was still snorkelling!

Oops! I'd done it again, as Britney would say! Only this time it wasn't my foot I'd put in it like I'd done in the travel agents, it was a *different* part of my body I'd put in it - my bell end! And I'd more or less put it in this bloke's face!

He looked like he'd swallowed half the ocean. He couldn't stop coughing seawater up and he was nearly choking gasping for breath! It must have really shook him up. Christ knows what he must have thought. There he was, minding his own business, happily snorkelling, looking at the marvellous array of beautiful fish, when all of a sudden a naked man swims past him waving his cock at him!

He started ranting and raving in Norwegian. Well it sounded Norwegian anyway. Whatever language it was he wasn't happy I know that! And he started swimming towards me. I've no idea what it was he was saying as I don't speak Norwegian though I'd imagine it was along the lines of, "I'll rip your knob OFF if I get my hands on you, you fucking idiot!" In any language it was clear he wasn't happy. He was built like a brick shithouse too, so off I swam. Very quickly! I was like Duncan Goodhew swimming back to the beach! I didn't half motor. *I* was coughing and spluttering and gasping for breath too by the time I got back to Andy, who, needless to say, thought it was hilarious when I told him what had happened.

But it was the night before I was due to fly on to Phuket to meet Andy and the others when I met the bloke who'd been 'given the chop' by his wife. It was in a bar in Bangkok and I was talking to the owner and he told me a story about one of the 'girls' he had working for him.

Quite a lot of the girls who work in bars in Thailand are, or used to be, men. But for one reason or another, mainly financial reasons so they can earn money in the bars, they decide to become a woman. Some go the whole hog and have their tackle surgically removed and have breast implants, while others keep their tackle and just have breasts implanted. In the main, those who hang on to their tackle after having breast implants do so because they can't afford the operation to have it removed, though a lot of them hang on to it because some men (tourists) like to have sex with a 'woman' who's got a cock - or a bloke who's got tits - depending on how you look at it, and they're willing to pay for it.

A lot of the 'women' in the bars really are stunning and some of them you can't tell the difference between a 'real' woman and a 'man-made' one; one that has had the old 'nip and tuck' down below, or the 'chop and lob' as it's known. The man-made ones *are* man-made too when you think about it because they were born as men! And there was one 'man-made' one that this bar owner pointed out to me who he had working in his bar who'd had the chop and lob himself. Only he didn't *choose* to have it done. His wife chopped his cock off for him. And then lobbed it. Over the edge of a cliff! And he never saw it again.

Unlike the wives in the previous stories who did what they did in a fit of rage and in a moment of madness, this fella's wife was more calculating.

After she found out that her husband was cheating on her with her best friend she didn't confront him about it she just pretended that she didn't know anything about it and just carried on as normal as though everything was fine. Then one day she suggested they go for a drive up into the mountains. And as they were driving up this long winding mountain road in the middle of nowhere that had a thousand foot drop at the side of it which went down into a ravine and a fast flowing river, she put her hand on her husband's crotch and starting rubbing it. She then smiled at him, and he smiled back. Little did he know that his smile would soon be wiped off his face - and replaced with a grimace. His wife then unzipped his fly's and took his cock out and leant forward and began to give him a blow job. And as her husband was driving along, gleefully having his cock sucked whilst taking in the picturesque views of the surrounding mountainside and no doubt glancing down at his wife thinking, "The daft cow has got no idea I've been shagging her best mate!" His wife, who knew *exactly* what he'd been doing, discretely took the sharp knife from under the driver's seat that she'd put there earlier, put the bladed edge against the base of his knob about an inch above his ball sack and sliced right through it. And not content with just cutting his knob completely off, she then wound the window down and lobbed it out, purposely throwing it over the edge of the mountain into the ravine and into the white-water rapids a 1000ft below!

At least John Wayne Bobbitt's wife gave him half a chance by just throwing his knob into a field so it could be retrieved. This fella's wife didn't. It was gone forever!

How bad must that have been for him? It'd have been surreal. Can you imagine seeing your own cock flying through the air in front of you and watching it disappear over the edge of a cliff! Fucking hell! It doesn't bear thinking about does it. And if his knob had bounced off the windscreen first it'd have been a bit like that joke in my Dropping Dad In It Story! Not that the bloke would've laughed. His wife wasn't laughing much in the end either as she got ten years in prison for doing it.

After it happened the fella unwittingly became the centre of attention and he became a bit of a local 'celebrity.' And when this bar owner suggested he could make money from his new found fame by working in his bar as a 'tourist attraction' he took him up on his offer. And so at night-time he'd put a long black wig on, slap a bit of make-up on, put on a short skirt and earn his living hoisting it up to flash what was left of his meat and two veg' to curious tourists like me! Well he flashed his two veg' anyway. He didn't have much meat left to flash. It was more like a mini sausage. The shrivelled sort you get on a cocktail stick at parties! And it wasn't much of a tourist attraction either to be honest. It was hardly 'The Big One' at Blackpool Pleasure Beach. It was more 'The Little One'. A *very* little one! One that was half the size of a fifty pence piece that it cost to look at!

But you don't have to go to the Far East to risk getting your knob chopped off by your missus, it could quite easily happen in this country too. And if 'Winny's' wife would have had a knife to hand when he did what he did to her *his* cock would also now resemble a mini sausage...

Horse name

Close Encounters Of The Turd Kind

Owner

Billy

Story behind the name

I used to buy and sell houses. I'd get them cheap, do them up and sell them again. And I'd get lads in that I knew to do the work for me. I say I'd get 'lads' in to do the work as a turn of phrase so to speak as they weren't really lads as such, they were grown men, some of whom were married. One of them was called Michael. He was a good bloke. He had a great sense of humour and he was funny, and I got on well with him. He was a good worker too though he did have one problem; he was forever shitting. He'd have at least six shit's a day. Some days he'd spend more time shitting than he would working!

He was a plasterer. He was *shit hot* at it too - that's if you could get him off the bastard toilet to put the plaster on the wall! He didn't have a bowel problem or have anything wrong with him medically that caused him to shit so much, and he didn't eat particularly excessively either which would have caused him to produce more shit, he just produced it! Though having said that he didn't have a bowel problem he obviously *did* have a problem with his bowels because no fucker has six shit's a day!

He hadn't been *diagnosed* with a bowel problem, put it that way. Though it's a pity he *hadn't* been diagnosed with one because if he had have been they may have fitted him with a colostomy bag and he could've carried on working whilst he shit. I must have paid him for three hours of the day just to sit on the bog!

People rarely called Michael by his first name. He had a nickname. He had *several* nicknames actually, one of them being 'Winny'. This was because his surname was *Winner*. He was also known as Winny The 'Poo', as in the honey eating bear. Can you guess why he was sometimes called this? Course you can! It was because he was always 'poo-ing', though he did slightly more than 'poo' whenever he went to the toilet. He'd have fucking massive dumps - and leave most of it splattered around the pan. However, 'Winny The Fucking Massive Dumping Pan Splatterer' was a bit long for a nickname so we settled for Winny The Poo instead.

He was also known as 'Death Wish'. Any guesses as to why he was also known as this? (Some of you older ones reading - and film buffs - will probably have guessed.) No idea? Well it wasn't because he wished to shit himself *to* death, though there was every chance he quite easily could have done considering how much he used to shit. And we often did *wish* he'd hurry up on the toilet when we needed to go ourselves. However the reason he was sometimes known as Death Wish was because he had the same name as the director of that film, Michael Winner.

How many of you knew that as well as being a film director Michael Winner was also a food critic? Well he was, and a very well renowned one at that. And I bet that if he'd have ever looked in the toilet after his namesake had just been and had seen the remnants of the food that Winny had left splattered all around the pan he'd have been highly fucking critical of that too! Like we all used to be! And so much like Winny's shit used to stick to the pan the nickname Winny The Poo stuck with him.

He used to fart and follow through all the time as well. He'd do it regularly and it became a standing joke. Many a time someone would asked, "Where's Winny gone?" And one of us would say, "He's gone to change his undies because he's followed through again!" He did it that often that he used to bring spare pairs of underpants to work with him. I'm not kidding either. Everyone else would bring a flask and a butty box to work, Winny would bring two packs of boxer shorts!

He'd also get 'caught short' and he'd get a sudden urge to have a crap and you'd see him legging it up the stairs to the toilet. He got caught short once in the van. It was the first week back after Christmas and we were on a retail park having a McDonalds before we went into Wickes to get a few bits that we needed. We were then going on to the tip to dump some rubbish bags from the job that we had in the back of the van. Also in the back of the van were some bags of my own, bin bags that I'd brought from home that had the empty boxes from Christmas presents in them along with other stuff that had piled up over Christmas, and I was getting rid of those at the tip too. And one of the boxes proved to come in very handy, and it just so happened that it'd come from a shop on that retail park.

As we were sat in the van eating our McDonalds, Winny said, "Is there a bucket in the back?" So I said, "There is, yeah. Why?" And he said, "Because I need a crap," so I said, "You can fuck off! You're not shitting in the van," and told him that he'd have to hold it in until we got back on the job. And he said, "I don't think I *can* hold it in. I'm dying for one." So I said, "Well you're gonna fucking have to because you're not shitting in here!"

So we carried on eating our Big Mac's - which I'd suddenly lost my appetite for at the thought of Winny emptying his bowels in a bucket next to me - and as I'm looking across the car park I saw these two scrotes walking up to parked cars and looking in the windows and trying the door handles to see if they were open.

They were 'on the rob' - thieving.

Winny had clocked them as well and he said to me, "Look at them two fuckers." So I said, "I know. I've seen 'em." And as we sat there watching them trying the door handles on all the cars an idea sprung to mind and I got out of the van and went and got one of the boxes I'd brought from home that was in the back.

It was the box from a MacBook that I'd bought my eldest daughter for Christmas. I'd got it from Argos that we were parked more or less opposite of. I nearly had a fucking heart attack too when I bought it and the assistant said it was £999.

A grand! For one bleeding Christmas present! I used to get The Beano Annual and a tangerine in a stocking for Christmas when I was a kid!

So I gave the box to Winny and said, "Here. Get in the back and shit in that and leave it on the passenger seat." And he started laughing and said, "Fucking great idea!"

I told him to leave the van doors open after he'd done it and to meet me at the entrance to Wickes, which was just across the car park. And so as I walked over to Wickes, Winny got in the back of the van and filled the box to the brim with shit. He then put the lid down on it so it looked as though it was unopened and put it on the front seat and walked over to where I was, and we stood just out of sight watching these two lads.

A couple of minutes later they walked up to the van. They tried the back doors of the van first of all, probably thinking that the van would have tools in it, and when they found that it was unlocked they opened one of the doors and put their heads in to have a look.

I'm surprised they didn't throw up when they stuck their heads in - knowing what Winny's shits are like it must've fucking stank in there!

They saw that it was just full of rubbish, and so seeing that there was nothing worth nicking they closed the doors and walked around to the front of the van and peered through the passenger window, and they both immediately looked at each other as though they couldn't quite believe their own eyes when they saw what was lying on the front seat: a thousand pound Apple MacBook that someone must have just bought from PC World opposite, sitting there waiting to be taken by some thieving little bastards. So the thieving little bastards opened the passenger door and took it! And ran off with it.

Oh and how me and Winny pissed ourselves laughing watching them run across the car park with it!

They must have been thinking, "Yippee! A top of the range laptop! We'll get a few quid for this!" Only what they had *wasn't* top of the range. It was a load of crap! They may not have got away with any *tools* from the van though they did get several *stools*! I'd loved to have been a fly on the wall when they opened it. And there was probably quite a few fly's circulating around the box when they did!

That was probably the only occasion where I was quite pleased that Winny couldn't control his bowels, although those two scrotes weren't the only ones to cop for a pile of Winny's turds as a result of him not being able to control his bowel movements. Someone else once copped for a pile of Winny's turds too when he lost control of his bowels on another occasion. His wife. Only she didn't cop for them in a box like those two thieving bastards did, she copped for them right in her mush, and she wasn't at all pleased when she copped for them!

At some time or another when getting a blow job off their wife it would have crossed most bloke's minds to fart in her face whilst she's doing it. Just for a laugh! Few blokes ever do it though because they know that if they *did* do it it'd probably be the last blow job they ever got off their wife. It may also result in them suffering the same fate as John Wayne Bobbitt and co' because their wife would probably bite their cock off right there and then! And just like any wives reading would've said that they'd have rammed the tin of pears down their husband's throats if their husband had told them to get back home and open the tin for them, I'm sure all wives reading will also be thinking, "If my fucking husband ever farted in *my* face whilst I was giving him a blow job I'd fucking kill the bastard!"

But when you think about it, women quite often break wind in their husband's face during oral sex, yet we don't hit the roof when they do it to us do we? How many times have you gone down on your wife and as you're licking and flicking the bean and slipping a couple of fingers in and out she lets out a massive fanny fart. Right in your kisser! It's the same thing innit! Fair enough, the wind doesn't come from their arses and it doesn't stink like a fart does, but a wife letting out a squelching wet fanny fart in her husband's face whilst *he's* going down on *her* is no different than a husband blasting a fart in his wife's face whilst *she's* going down on *him*!

And blokes do think about doing it. When you're lying there on the bed looking at the top of your wife's head bobbing up and down you can't help but think, "Wouldn't it be funny if I let rip now!" And the same thought crossed Winny's mind one night when his wife was giving him a nosh. And he did it! And he said it was a real blaster that he let out. The only problem was - the problem being for his wife - was that it wasn't just wind that flew out. Numerous turds came flying out as well!

He told us about it the following day in work. He said that he 'only' meant to fart in his wife's face but he followed through as well and turd after turd shot out of his arse like ballistic missiles and splattered in his wife's face! Not surprisingly, *his wife* then went ballistic!

I once did a similar thing, although when *I* did it the girl I did it to didn't go ballistic at me she apologised! Though she didn't cop for it in the face like Winny's wife did, she copped for it from the neck downwards. Right down to her ankles!

It happened when I was on holiday in Benidorm with a few of my mates. I'd had a bit of 'Spanish Tummy' as they call it. I had the shits in other words! I'd had it for a few days prior to it happening and I'd followed through twice already on the day of the night it happened. The first time I followed through that day wasn't too bad as I did it when I was swimming in the sea. I farted and a load of diarrhoea shot out. There was loads of it too. It was like an oil slick had appeared! Luckily no-one was near me so I just washed it off and carried on swimming. The second time I wasn't so lucky though because it happened in a crowded beach bar as I was queuing to get served and EVERYONE saw it. And *did I* get the piss taken out of me! Everyone was pissing themselves laughing and pointing at me. I felt a right cunt! The only plus point of it happening was that a big gap opened up around me and I walked right up to the bar and got served straight away!

Anyhow, that night I ended up back at this girl's apartment and we were in bed and she was giving me a tit wank. She was lying on her back and I was sat with my knees either side of her, straddling her, with my cock in between her tits, and as she was rubbing her tits up and down over my knob I could feel my guts churning and bubbling and I really wanted to fart but I knew that if I did I'd follow through. Half of me wanted to do it for a giggle, but the other half of me didn't. It was like I had the Devil on one shoulder and an Angel on the other and the Devil was saying, "Go on. Do it! You know you want to. It'll be funny. And your mates will think it's fucking hilarious when you tell them!" And the Angel was saying, "No! Don't even *think* about doing it!"

In the end I didn't listen to the Devil *or* the Angel. The choice for me to do it was made for me by the girl herself who without warning, and without asking if I'd mind, suddenly stuck her finger up my arse which took me completely by surprise and made me shoot up in the air. And as I did so her finger came out which triggered a humungous fart - one that sounded like a Whoopee cushion factory exploding! This was then followed by a loud gushing noise as a tidal wave of rusty coloured watery shit flew out of my arsehole and plastered the girl from head to toe! But instead of going mental like Winny's wife did she jumped off the bed and started apologising to me! Which seemed a bit strange; *I'd* just shit all over *her* yet *she* was apologising to *me*! She just stood there, looking like someone had just squirted a dozen bottles of HP sauce all over her - or that my dad had just poured a bottle of his Camp coffee over her! - and all she kept saying was, "I'm so sorry! I'm so sorry!" Well I suppose it was her own fault for sticking her finger up my hole! Talking of which, another incident that I participated in that involved a hole and a pile of my own shit took place on a local golf course the day before I was sent to prison. Although the golfer who unwittingly participated in this 'joke' was far from apologetic like the girl in Benidorm was. He didn't see the funny side to the joke either.

It was mine and a mate of mine's (Rob) last night of 'freedom'. It was a Saturday night and on the Monday morning we were at crown court where we knew, having been told by our barrister, that we'd be spending a bit of time at her majesty's pleasure. The thought of which didn't *give us* much pleasure! So we decided to have one last blow out.

It was the middle of summer and after we'd been to a nightclub we ended up at a house party which we left at about five o'clock in the morning. We walked home through a local country park and on the way we sat down on a little hill that overlooked the local golf course, and right in front of us was the third green. It was around 5.30am by now and with it being summer it was light and in the distance we could see four golfers about to tee off at the first hole. Rob noticed some dog shit and said should we put it in the hole and see if one of them picks it up when they get their ball out. Childish I know. But then again so is shitting in MacBook boxes and leaving them lying around for car thieves to take, and chuckling at the thought of farting in your wife's face whilst she's giving you a blow job! So we thought, 'Fuck it. We'll do it!' So we picked the dog shit up with a bit of cardboard, went down the slope, climbed through a gap in the fence that surrounded the golf course and walked over to the green to put it in the hole. But then similar to how when I saw the two car thieves on the retail park and an idea came to mind, as Rob was about to put the dog crap in the hole a thought *also* came to mind. So I said to him, "Hang on. I've got a better idea," and I took the flag out, took down my jeans, squatted over the hole and had a shit in it. I then put the flag back in the hole took off my underpants, wiped my arse with them and hung them on the flag! We then went back and sat on the hill opposite.

We watched the golfers tee off at the first hole and half an hour or so later they played their shots onto the green in front of us. As they walked onto the green one of them walked up to the hole to take the flag out and he noticed the undies hanging on them and he shouted to his mates, "Some dirty fucker has hung their shitty undies on the flag!" And they all started laughing and the bloke flicked the undies off the flag and then laid the flag at the side of the green, not noticing that it had shit on the other end of it.

His mate then took his putter out and played his shot from about fifteen yards away and his ball rolled and stopped about a foot from the edge of the hole. It was a pretty good shot, though it would turn out to be a *shitty* good shot! He then strode up to his ball and tapped it in and then bent down to pick it up from out of the hole. And as he went to pick it up Rob shouted over to him, "Nice shit…..I mean *SHOT*!"

It was perfect timing because it momentarily distracted the bloke who glanced up at us as he leant forward to reach for his ball. We were trying not to laugh as he looked at us and we thought he'd look down again into the hole as he picked his ball out. But he didn't. Instead, he shouted back, "Cheers mate," and at the same time he put his hand in the hole and picked up his ball. And picked up a handful of my shit with it! And as he stood up he realised that he had something sticky on his fingers and all over his hand and he looked down at it to see what it was. He then looked in the hole and lifted his hand to his face and sniffed his fingers. That's when he realised what it was and he shouted, "The fucking dirty cunts!"

One of his mates said, "What's up?" And the bloke replied, "Someone's had a shit in the fucking hole and I've got it all over my fucking hand!"

Me and Rob burst out laughing and he looked over at us and shouted, "Have you cunts done that?" And Rob replied, "No, I think it was a *birdie*!" And *I* shouted, "Though looking at the size of the turd in that hole I think it must have been an *Eagle* or an *Albatross*!" (names of golf shots.) And added, "But don't worry. You can wipe your hand on my undies. It's okay, I don't want 'em back!" And the bloke shouted, "You fucking dirty pair of bastards!" and then all four of them reached into their golf bags for their drivers and took them out and started belting golf balls at us! They were shit shots too because none of them hit us!

I've never played golf in my life, although I don't mind watching it now and then when it's on tele', in particular the US Master's from Augusta. I enjoy watching that as much for the scenery as I do for the golf. Some of the backdrops, such as the flower displays on the holes behind the bunkers like those on the 13th green are amazing. I also use to enjoy listening to Peter Alliss commentating. He was quite funny, although some (the PC brigade and those with no sense of humour) said that he was a little bit 'inappropriate' at times with some of the things he came out with, though for most it made what he said even funnier! Sadly, Peter Alliss died in December 2020.

But isn't it weird that even though you don't play golf you always seem to come across a golf ball in your garage that you never knew you had? I also once found a golf club in the garage that I never knew I had. God knows where that came from because like I say, I've never played golf in my life. But wherever it came from it did come in handy one night. And that's because not only have I found golf clubs and golf balls in my garage that I didn't realise

I had in there, I once found a burglar in my garage that I didn't realise was in there! And I don't know who was more startled at first, him or me. *I* was certainly startled when I walked in and saw a hooded figure standing there rooting around seeing what he could pinch. Though I think *he* was ten times more startled when he turned around and saw me standing there stark bollock naked!

The reason I was naked was because I'd just got out of the shower and I realised my towel was downstairs in the utility room so I went downstairs to get it. (My wife and kids were out just in case you were wondering - I don't usually walk around the house naked!) And as I went into the utility room I heard a noise in the garage next to it and when I opened the door I saw him. And he saw me; standing there with my knob dangling down. (All twelve inches of it!!!)

It must have been a pretty frightening sight for him too because not only was I fully naked I was also full of steroids. I was bang into bodybuilding at the time and I was 16st of solid muscle, and I had a skin head too! I used to look a right thug!

He must have been absolutely petrified when he saw me standing there naked. I'll never forget the look on his face, he must have been thinking, "Is this bloke going to make a citizen's arrest or bugger me!" I did neither. I picked up the golf club and fucking battered him with it!

Squatting over that hole on the golf course and having a crap in it was good practice for what was to come, because after going to crown court on the Monday morning I spent the next eight months squatting over a bucket to have a crap! I wasn't particularly looking forward to going to prison, I could think of better ways of spending eight months of my life that's for sure.

Though our sentence was nothing compared to some of the sentences that some blokes I met in there were serving. Eight months was no more than a 'shit and a shave' as the saying goes to describe a short spell in prison and considering what the last few pages have been about that saying is probably quite an appropriate one to use to bring this story to an end!

Horse name

Snatch Of The Day

Owner

Billy

Story behind the name

When I was in Thailand one of the bars that we used to go in was a football themed bar and all the 'girls' - it was hard to tell which were and which weren't girls unless they lifted up their skirt and flashed their mini sausage at you! - wore English teams football shirts. And it gave me an idea for a bit of a wind up. On Gary Lineker! And when I got back home I wrote to his agent. This is what I emailed him:

Dear Sir,

I represent a production company called Up The Wrong 'Un and we were wondering if your client, Gary Lineker, would be interested in making a series of short video's called *Snatch* Of The Day which we plan to pitch to the BBC for them to show at the end of *Match* Of The Day. The idea is that every week at the end of the programme an attractive page three type model wearing only a thigh length premiership football shirt, and nothing else, comes on and stands in-between Gary and the two pundits, say, Alan Shearer and Ian Wright. Gary then introduces her and says, "And this week's snatch of the day is Tracy from Tottenham," or whichever football shirt the model is wearing. Gary then lifts up the model's shirt and shows the viewers her snatch. He then has a quick look at her minge, turns and smiles at the camera and says, "Nice tackle!" And that's all he has to do. However, as we comply with the equal opportunities law and we firmly believe in gender equality, every other week we plan to have a Ladyboy on the show. Would Gary be okay lifting up the shirt of a Ladyboy and saying he thinks she has nice tackle? And perhaps give her todger a quick flick like he's playing Subbuteo with it?

Kind regards,

A Numpty

Believe it or not his agent replied! Though all he put was, "No. He wouldn't be interested. And don't email me again!"

Three

The Winner's Enclosure

Horse name

Jumping For Joy

Owner

Ivan!

Story behind the name

As I mentioned at the beginning of the book I have a bet on the horses more or less every day. I don't put a lot of money on, just a fiver or so. I do the same bet, a fifty pence Yankee which costs £5.50. I win a few quid here and there but nothing worth writing home about as they say. But one day I changed my bet and this *is* worth writing about!

Though if it wasn't for Graham I *wouldn't* be writing about it.

I went in the bookies one morning and Graham was in there and he said, "Any luck yesterday?" meaning had I won anything. So I said, "Yes. Mostly bad! I had one winner and three 2$^{nd's}$." So he said, "Why don't you do the bet that I do for a change. An each way accumulator and an each way accumulator E – D (equally divided.) And he said, "At least that way if you get a couple of winners and a couple of placed horses you'll get something back."

So I asked him what the most was he'd ever won doing that bet and he said that he once won £450 and I thought well that's not bad. So I said I'd give it a go and instead of picking out four horses like I usually do when I put a Yankee on I picked out six, which were:

Gabriel The Tiger
KeepUp Kevin
Kilbaha Lady
EverKyllachy
So Lonely
Three Colours Red

I put on a £1 e/w acc' and a £1 e/w acc' E-D (doing it equally divided works in your favour if you get a mixture of winner's and placed horses) and I chatted with Graham for ten minutes and left. And as I was leaving he jokingly shouted, "And don't forget my commission for telling you about the bet if it comes up!" So I said, "Don't worry. I will. But don't hold your breath. You know what my luck's like!"

However Graham *could've* held his breath because my luck was about to change. And I was nearly *gasping* for breath later that night when I checked my horses.

I check my horses the 'old fashioned' way. I do it on TeleText! (BBC One page 300) Nowadays everyone's got apps on their phones or do it online but I prefer TeleText. (I still book my holidays on TeleText!) I was sat on the sofa and I checked the first one, Gabriel The Tiger and saw that it had won at 11/2. "Good start," I thought to myself. I checked the second one, KeepUp Kevin. That won too at 5/2. Two out of two! Two out of two then became three out of three when I saw that Kilbaha Lady had also won, at 4/1.

I then started to get a little bit excited and when I checked the fourth horse, EverKyllachy, and saw that had won as well at 9/2 I began to get VERY excited! But as anyone who backs horses will tell you, even though you're excited at the thought that you're bet is going to come up you've always got that doubt that it won't.

And in the back of your mind you're thinking, "The next one will let me down. It always does. I'm not that lucky." But in this instance the next one, So Lonely, *didn't* let me down. It won at 7/4! "Jesus!!" I thought. "Could it be!"

I did a quick calculation of the odds and worked out that I had around £1,600 going on the last horse, Three Colours Red. I was shitting myself! I didn't want to check it! I COULDN'T check it at first I was that nervous!

I'm not quite sure why I did this because it just made the drama, suspense, nerves and excitement even worse. But I shouted to my two kids and my wife who were upstairs to come down and I told them that when I switched to the page that had the result on it to tell me how many words the winning horse had in it but not to say the name of it. So I switched the page over and at the same time I looked away from the screen and said, "How many words are in the horse's name?" And they said, "3." Now my nerves *were* jangling! I then drew it out even more and put myself through *even more* torture and said, "What's the first letter of the first word and they said, "T". I then said, "What's the first letter of the second word. "C" came the reply - and my nerves started jangling ten times more than what they already were! So I said, "And what's the first letter of the *third* word?"

The moment was spoilt slightly at this point when my eldest tutted and said to me, "Just look at the screen you Dickhead!" But I *couldn't* look. I daren't! So I said, "Don't call your Dad a dickhead. Even though I am one! Just tell me the letter," and at the same time they all said, "It's R." I was then 99.9% certain that my bet had come up. So I said, "Is it called Three Colours Red?" And they said, "Yes."

BINGO!!! My bet had come up! But I still didn't look at the tele.

Instead, and finally, much to my eldest's relief! I said, "Next to the horse's name are some numbers. What are they?" And my youngest said, "It's got a 10 with a line beside it and then a 1."

"No way?!" I gasped loudly! And I looked at the screen and saw that it had won at 10/1 "I've won sixteen grand!!" I shouted! And I jumped off the sofa and started dancing around the room like an idiot. Or like a Dickhead!

It actually turned out to be just over £20,000 I'd won, though it would have been over £23,000 if wasn't for a 'rule four' which impacts the odds if one of the horses in the race is withdrawn. But still, I was happy with twenty grand!

The next day I went in the bookies and cashed it in. They obviously didn't pay that amount in cash so they transferred £17,000 into my bank account using my bank-card and I took £3,000 in cash. I hung around for Graham and when he came in he asked me how my bet went on and I said, "I won twenty," and he said, "Well at least you're sixteen quid up. You only put £4 on didn't you?" He then laughed and said, "I'm not going to get any commission out of that am I!" And I said, "No. But you are out of twenty grand. Because that's what I've won!" And I gave him two hundred and fifty quid! He didn't believe me at first until the girl behind the counter said, "He has!!" And he said, "You jammy bastard! Well done!!" And you know what he did then? He gave me the £250 back and said he didn't want it, and said, "It's *your* winnings. You keep it." And no matter how many times I insisted that he had it he wouldn't take it. He said, "Get me a pint instead." So as soon as the pubs opened that's what I did. Though it ended up costing me a lot more than £250 due to the fact that he drank like a fucking fish and we ended up going on the piss all day until about ten o'clock and then went for a curry and finished the night off at the casino! But it was worth every penny because Graham was a top bloke. And he's sadly missed.

My winning betting slip!

That I had a good night out with Graham on...

SLIP	STAKE	TAX	TOTAL	STRUCK
564202108712	4.00	0.00	4.00	29 May 2019 11:54:11

GABRIAL THE TIGER	2.40 BEVERLEY	11/2	1/5	1-3	1st
KEEPUP KEVIN	3.10 BEVERLEY	5/2	1/5	1-3	1st
KILBAHA LADY	4.10 BEVERLEY	4/1	1/4	1-2	1st
EVERKYLLACHY	5.25 HAMILTON	9/2	1/5	1-3	1st
				R4 15p	
SO LONELY	7.40 WARWICK	7/4	1/4	1-2	1st
THREE COLOURS RED	8.45 WARWICK	10/1	1/4	1-2	1st

2 X	1.00	E/W	SIXFOLD		2.00
				Returns	16658.47
2 X	1.00	EQ DIVD	SIXFOLD		2.00
				Returns	3763.78

SLIP RETURNS	VOIDS	TOTAL
20422.25	0.00	20422.25

And my wife and kids spent most of the rest!

Printed in Great Britain
by Amazon